PELICAN BOOKS

BETRAYAL OF INNOCENCE

Susan Forward, M. S. W., is a licensed clinical social worker
specializing in intensive group psychotherapy and the training
of mental health professionals in the treatment of incest. She
is on the staff of Van Nuys Psychiatric Hospital and Ross
Loos Medical Center. She also serves as a consultant to the
San Fernando Valley Child Abuse Council, the Center for
the Improvement of Child Care and the Foundation for
Educational Services, among other public and private organi-
zations. Ms Forward has two children and lives in Los
Angeles.

Craig Buck is a freelance writer and journalist living in Los
Angeles. His work has appeared in numerous newspapers and
national magazines, and he has been a contributing writer
to several books, including *It's Your Body: A Woman's Guide
to Gynecology, The People's Almanac* and *The Rand McNalley
Traveler's Almanac.*

BETRAYAL

SUSAN FORWARD AND CRAIG BUCK

OF

INCEST AND ITS DEVASTATION

INNOCENCE

WITH AN INTRODUCTION BY DR JOHN GORDON

PENGUIN BOOKS

Penguin Books Ltd, Harmondsworth, Middlesex, England
Penguin Books, 625 Madison Avenue, New York, New York 10022, U.S.A.
Penguin Books Australia Ltd, Ringwood, Victoria, Australia
Penguin Books Canada Ltd, 2801 John Street, Markham, Ontario Canada L3R 1B4
Penguin Books (N.Z.) Ltd, 182–190 Wairau Road, Auckland 10, New Zealand

First published in the U.S.A. by J. P. Tarcher, Inc., 1978
Published simultaneously in Canada by Macmillan of Canada
This revised edition first published in Pelican Books 1981

The authors and publisher would like to thank Ann Landers,
the Field Newspaper Syndicate, and the Los Angeles Herald-Examiner
for permission to use a letter from Ann Landers' column.

Made and printed in Great Britain by
Richard Clay (The Chaucer Press) Ltd,
Bungay, Suffolk
Filmset in Monophoto Ehrhardt by
Northumberland Press Ltd, Gateshead, Tyne and Wear

CONTENTS

ACKNOWLEDGMENTS

There are many friends, colleagues, and advisors who guided us through this book. To them we offer thanks.

One man whom we found invaluable for moral and theoretical support is Merril B. Friend, M.D.

We are also grateful to the following for their contributions of time, energy, and information: Roland Summit, M.D., Lee Bloom, M.D., Hon. Peter Giannini, Referee Julius Libow, Alan Pollack, M.D., Jean E. Matusinka, Philip Moser, Sgt. Carol Walker, Sgt. Miriam Travis, Jolly K., Norris Paulson, Ph.D., Anne Chaleff, R. N., Ann Robbins, R. N., Clara Lowry, M. S. W., Ron Davis, Bernard A. Penziner, Hank Giarretto, Gertrude Bacon, Martin Erdman, Peter Ward, John Burton, Sandra Buck, Maxine Matthews, Toni L. Rubin, Kerry Stein, and Sarah Elliot.

To Victoria Pasternack, our editor, who directed our ascent from chaos, and to Jeremy Tarcher, who had the courage to publish this book, we give special thanks.

But the people who really deserve the most credit for this book are the many family members who have been involved in incest and were brave enough to share their stories here. Without them, this book would not be.

INTRODUCTION

The temptations and riddles presented to us in the universal love we bear for our mothers, fathers, brothers, sisters and the intimates of our childhood – love which may turn to hate but is rarely numbed into indifference – are the subject of this contemporary American study. In particular, the book illustrates ways through the pain and deadly guilt which may ensue in our culture when the temptation to possess each other sexually within the conventional family, other than as husband and wife, is not resisted.

Incestuous sex is much more common than we imagine. It is usually kept dark and secret. Family secrets which we do not at any price want to admit even to ourselves influence our every meeting with another person and are a source of hindrance and confusion to many of us.

Family relationships form a child in spite of secrets, and, through the form, beget the future of civilization. That is what is at stake. If civilization be destroyed (it may be destroyed if there be too many sinister secrets amongst us) even then we hope our children may be able to recognize the truth enough to find their way, and find life, with whomsoever they may. The responsibility of parenthood, in which we all partake, whether or not we have children, is awesome. The growth of children is a source of wonder and reverence to us all. In spite of us they love and play and create, and in due course will beget children of their own. If our love for our little children be possessive, we hinder the very kingdom of heaven nascent within each of them. To everyone, in their hearts, parenthood implies guardianship, care without burden or attachment, love without bonds, stewardship, and the joy and privilege of being for twelve to twenty years of our life with those souls most intimately given into our care and engendered through our fucking. Each of those who are children to us may be lost unless we nurture them attentively and allow them to find their way. But devilment and hell would sometimes have us force them and control, dictate and possess them, even bind them, even in the name of friendship, without an ear to their complaint, without knowing what we are doing.

Today I heard a baby crying in the street underneath my window. 'Stop crying! Stop! Stop it!' ordered the father. As I listened, it embarrassed him in front of all the imaginary people round about who seemed to tell him how painful it was to have a child crying. The child winced and turned in silent hopelessness to his mother, who walked on. 'You horrid person!' I thought, of the father, 'You never listen to the cry! Your wife looks as though she hears it but seems to go along with you to please you. She longs to please you for she loves you, I can see, and has committed herself to having your children. She loves that infant's cry and would respond to it if such behaviour were not uncivilized in our male society, and therefore a nuisance to women who want to make it with men like you. Weep, child, weep! Let us hear it! Let us hear your cry in ourselves! Then we may cry to God!'

We all long to belong to each other; parents and children, all of us, long to be human in a human world, to be recognized and loved, cries and warts and all, to be allowed space in which to grow together. Some of us, some of our children, may seem very peculiar, may hurt and embarrass us. We may not understand them, and they may cry when least convenient and least expected. We are often tempted not to allow those who embarrass us or whom we do not understand to belong amongst us; but we ignore them at our peril, and to abuse them is murderous.

Our baby's cry may resonate with a hidden cry within ourselves, a cry we may never want to hear. We can avoid the resonance if we force our child to stop crying. But how, then, can our child's cry, and our denied scream, belong?

Would we leave people all about us with parts of themselves not belonging, inhuman, monstrous, with their guts hanging out, as it were, just because it is inconvenient or because we do not understand? If there be too much that is patently human yet never allowed to belong – if there be too many suppressed cries – it will all some day erupt with terrible violence. That time of war may be coming quickly again. We are ignoring what we would rather not hear at our very peril. As we suppress it, lock it away, file it away, murder it, we write our own death-warrants.

We live in a desperate age, and we must listen to what we would at all costs avoid hearing, or perish with our children. We must listen to each other more. If we listen, God speaks and the spirit moves in spite of us.

In our confusion at trying to avoid what we should rather not hear from our child, we may find ourselves insisting, in spite of ourselves, that in order to belong with us our child must seem to be our friend and intimate, our 'mate.' 'Be my mate then I shall not have to listen to your cry, and to its resonance in me, any more.' Our child longs to belong, and would bend over backwards not to be lost, not to freak us or himself into a state where all seems lost, where all sustenance of family vanishes in the dark abyss. Our child is then thrown into utter purgatory: he can either make love with us and be sucked into the hell of being taken over, possessed, or he may, of course, hate us and leave, which is also hell. To do either is terrifying; he will lose himself either way. His cry and prayer can only be 'deliver me from evil' – and, if anyone would look at his face or hear him, that is just what he is saying. We fail to hear that sort of cry at our very peril, for God works through us and we cannot afford to ignore it when we are so moved.

Our child may well settle for intimacy and friendship with one or both or all of us, and deny his cry, in order to seem to belong. 'After all, why not?' he may say to himself. If he is lucky, our child may hate us when we make these conditions for him, and that hate can be his release, his chance if he will ask someone who hears. Most do not hate like that for they cannot allow themselves to see clearly enough, or have not been able to hold on to themselves or let go of it all. Most will not take that leap of faith. Most kids would allow themselves to be possessed as a seeming belonging within that familial intimacy and friendship. That is incest.

If expression be quite often given to such possession in sexual intimacy, it is hardly surprising. It will happen most frequently when inhibitions are dissolved in alcohol, when we can more easily say 'after all, why not?' and ignore our salvation.

When we possess each other, or anything else on earth, in order to enable us to ignore and disallow what we do not want to hear, we are deluded and lost, just as lost as our violated children. (Of course, we may deny that what we do not want to hear is there at all, for it does not appear to us if we do not hear it – but is it there if we *listen*?) We may frantically try not to be lost by indulging in every earthly pleasure. After all, this or that or the other may for a moment assuage our painful desire. But then it is not difficult for others to see, underneath the glamour, a frenzy, sleepless anxiety, guilt and dread. If we are lucky, the truth of what is happening, of what we are doing and of what we have done, may dawn, and with that recognition comes life – we may find ourselves reborn and finding our way in good spirit! The pain of that recognition disappears in merciful forgiveness if we ask for it. Forgiveness is divine.

The guilt of the child who has allowed himself to be used appears, in experience, to be the more immediate and desperate. He or she is full of pains (may even be quite psychotic and unable to allow any of it). It may seem, after all we have been saying, that his only crime was that the child could find no one to hear his prayer: 'deliver me from evil.' But no! He knows he wanted to be taken in, *wanted* what he is now so guilty about. Not only that, he knows he bent over backwards to play his parents' game in order to survive at 'home' without war or having to go away. In this way he helped them not to face what they had done, and so he carries their guilt too. He also knows that part of him went away in consequence. He may even feel guilty for feeling utterly in pieces. All that makes for quite a tangle, quite a knot in every movement.

Throughout the ages, the answer to guilt has been confession; but confession of this sort of tangle is laborious and can hardly ever be made without the help of someone else in untangling it. Some priests, some physicians and some therapists, some grandmothers and some people one just meets can offer the foothold which makes sense. Sense of the common sort is that by which we find our way through whatever tangles have to be gone through. Sense is that by which we are moved and find our path. As we are moved on our way with others, we can ask forgiveness of God and include our parents and ourselves in our prayers, and may then make the most of the scars and loves we are left with.

Of course, sexual desires are in play all the time in a family, and the play is often enjoyed with various humour. Can we not allow that this is so? Fucking within a family sometimes begets children, and such children must be very precious. Far more usually, however, any delightful fantasy of possessing father, mother, brother, sister or grandfather, etc., yields to horror, dread and guilt when opportunity actually presents itself; for then there appears the hell of being taken over, of being possessed, of being sucked into a hellish game of denial in spite of oneself, of bending over backwards to please and losing all footholds.

In one manner or another, through dreams and substitutions, we all seem to endeavour, in spite of ourselves, to come to terms with the *idea* of fucking with our parent and sibling of the opposite sex and of the same sex. Such issues are disagreeable and mostly we should rather forget about them, but they remain under the surface. Their story is told vividly in Greek and other mythology, for example in the stories of Oedipus and of Phaedra. We may not be able to allow that such events could happen, or we may secretly not be able to allow that they could not happen, or both. Coming to terms with such forbidden ideas involves freeing oneself from any possession of or by one's family. Then we may even enjoy our family.

Our preference for keeping such matters taboo gives specialists 'material' to study incest as a 'problem,' and to 'treat' it if they possibly can. I guess that many of us have at some time or other actually known – whether we know it or not – some child of an incestuous fucking, and we may well have known some of the social play there was about it. Why, then, should we become so sophisticated as to consider it a 'problem' and so arrogant as to apply 'treatment'? We respond from our guts with abhorrence to violence, if violence there be. Moral judgement we may not apply, for we are all guilty of incest in one way or another, and have all desired physically to possess our mothers – every baby wants that!

Mostly, we prefer to forget that incestuous physical sex ever happened or ever occurred to us, and that we ignorantly or innocently pursued our ends in the lust of the moment. But guilt lingers and festers in spite of all we may do to avoid it. We may become ignorantly violent, in spite of ourselves, in order to avoid facing our guilt. But then to whom shall we confess it? Who will listen without judgement? It seems essentially to be the violence of ignorance, of one person ignoring another and not hearing what it hurts to hear, in order to protect himself, that begets 'problems' and 'treatment' and 'punishment.'

I have not heard that treatment or punishment have ever altered the incidence of violence and ignorance. At most, our attempts to treat and punish are bureaucratic in that they serve to file or hide or lock away those who are violent and wretched. Our prisons and mental hospitals, and our filing cabinets, are very full. Philanthropists, particularly in recent history, have made recommendations for education or psychotherapy as treatment, as though we should all benefit if we were made to hear of better things or were made to talk to specialists of our wretchedness. All too often this approach, too, serves to hide away the hell we do not want to hear of – to hide it away in specialist and academic systems – so that the rest of us may consider it all dealt with and need not bother about what we do not want to hear about.

Can we not listen? Why do we refuse to listen? We, all of us, listen with the desire of our very hearts but we get embarrassed when we are moved lest we be thought foolish. We ignore what moves us at our peril! In our embarrassment, we may become incestuous, may betray innocence and hinder experience. We only begin to know what we are doing if we *listen*.

February 1980   JOHN GORDON

I · BETRAYAL OF INNOCENCE

I understand incest not only as a psychotherapist but as a victim. When I was fifteen my father's playful seductiveness turned into highly sexualized fondling. This is a difficult admission for me to make, but even more painful is the fact that I enjoyed my father's attentions.

I felt enormously guilty about my participation in the incest, as if I had been responsible. I know now I was not. It was my father's responsibility as an adult and as a parent to prevent sexual contact between us, but I didn't understand that at the time.

I also felt guilty about competing with my mother – who was only thirty-three and very attractive.

I was flattered by my father's attraction to me, and his caresses felt good, but after several months my guilt became too great. I somehow found the courage to tell him to stop, and he did. The psychological damage, however, had already been done.

As my guilt feelings accumulated my self-image deteriorated. I felt like a 'bad girl'. I began to punish myself unconsciously, most prominently by marrying an unloving man instead of pursuing the acting career I had dreamed of since I was five. Later, when my children were in school, I finally got a job on a television series. Good jobs followed and success was within my grasp. But my guilt still fought me on an unconscious level, telling me that I didn't deserve success. So I allowed myself – unconsciously, of course – to become overweight and matronly at twenty-eight. My acting career stagnated. My marriage was a mess. I was desperately unhappy. Yet I had absolutely no idea that there was any connection between what my father had done to me and the problems in my life.

I finally sought professional help, and after only a few sessions of psychotherapy I made that connection. With time I put the pieces together and my life began to take a constructive direction. I divorced my husband; I learned to stop punishing myself; and I began to like myself.

My father had, by that time, also gone through extensive therapy, and we were able to come to terms with what had happened between us. I forgave him long before his death. That was important to him, but even more important to me. I could finally put the experience behind me.

After a few more years of acting I began to feel alienated from the people and lifestyle of show business, wanting to do something more personally fulfilling. Heeding a lifelong fascination for psychology I went to work as a volunteer at the Neuropsychiatric Institute at the University of California, Los Angeles, and a few years later enrolled in the University of Southern California's Graduate School of Social Work and obtained my master's degree. As I began working with therapy groups and honing my techniques, I knew I had finally found my place. Since then I have conducted more than ten thousand group therapy sessions, and have trained more than one thousand colleagues in group therapy techniques.

My work with the incest trauma grew out of my groups, because I was amazed at the number of patients who admitted during therapy sessions to having been incest victims. I have treated more than three hundred admitted incest cases in the last decade and I am sure many more had incest stories that they never found the courage to tell.

This work alone seemed sufficient to qualify me to write this book, so as the publisher's deadline for the manuscript approached I agonized over whether it was necessary to reveal my own incest. I had kept my experience carefully hidden from family and friends all my life; the thought of a sudden public admission was terrifying. I considered remaining secure behind my professional credentials, but I realized that if I were to persuade others to break through their walls of secrecy and shame, I had to be willing to do so myself.

TEN MILLION VICTIMS

This is not so much a book about incest as it is a book about people — all kinds of people. There are probably more than ten million Americans who have been involved in incest, and they come from every economic, cultural, racial, educational, religious, and geographical background.

They are doctors, policemen, prostitutes, secretaries, artists, and merchants. They are heterosexual, bisexual, and homosexual. They are happily married and four-times divorced. They are leading productive lives and they have been convicted of murder. They are emotionally stable and they have multiple personalities. In short, the people whose stories appear in this book have only one thing in common: incest.

Incest is not some freakish perversion confined to the back alleys of Marrakech; it is a fact of life that has involved at least one out of every twenty Americans. According to a 1969 study by the 'American Humane Association,' 'The problem of sexual abuse of children is of unknown national dimensions, but findings strongly point to the probability of an enormous national incidence *many times larger* than the reported incidence of physical abuse of children.' In other words, everything you've read about the battered-child epidemic amounts to only a fraction of the problem of incest.

Among the reported victims of incest girls outnumber boys by seven to one. Various studies estimate that up to one of every four women in the United States is a victim of sexual molestation by the time she reaches eighteen years of age. According to the Humane Association study 38 percent of these molestations are incestuous. That works out to one out of every ten women.

The figures cited are not consistent with each other; they are derived from imperfect research. But clearly the problem of incest is much more prevalent than most people realize or care to admit. The traditional estimate of one-in-a-million is no more than a wish.

A FAMILY PROBLEM

In this book I will be specifically concerned with the psychological implications of incest – the causes, consequences, and treatment. Because of this my definition of incest differs somewhat from the dictionary definition. *Webster's Third International Dictionary* defines incest as 'sexual intercourse or interbreeding between closely related individuals especially when they are related or regarded as related ... within degrees wherein marriage is prohibited by law or custom.' I define incest as any overtly sexual contact between people who are either closely related or perceive themselves to be closely related (including stepparents, stepsiblings, halfsibilings, and even live-in lovers if they have assumed a parental role). If that special trust that exists between a child and a parent-figure or sibling is violated by a sexual act, that act becomes incestuous. It makes no difference, for example, whether the aggressor is a natural father or a stepfather as long as the child perceives him to be 'daddy.'

When I discuss incest I am referring to an entire family picture, not just a sexual act. It would be easy to pin all the blame on the aggressor – the logical scapegoat – but easy solutions rarely apply in human relationships. In a typical father–daughter incest case the mother is frequently guilty of unconsciously pushing the daughter into a maternal role, and the daughter may be seductive. The father is ultimately responsible for acting out the incest, but he alone does not set it up. Incest generally develops in a troubled family. Rather than causing a breakdown in the family most incest is the result of such a breakdown. Family members are often emotionally isolated from one another and there is usually a good deal of loneliness and hostility before incest occurs. Unlike other sex crimes, incest is not merely the result of a perverted individual assaulting a random victim.

Because of this shared involvement, every family member suffers from incest – not just the victims. The fathers, mothers, grandfathers, step-parents, older siblings, and other incest aggressors and their spouses also suffer from incest. They come away with weighty guilts and feelings of inadequacy and sadness because the urges that drew them into the incestuous relationship have not been fulfilled. Incestuous victory is rarely sweet.

WHY A BOOK ON INCEST?

Everyone is touched by incest, not just those family members who are directly involved. Aside from the psychological and emotional effects of incest on the participants, incest affects society by driving some of the participants to prostitution, drug and alcohol abuse, violence, and a variety of other social problems. Incest is widespread and costly in many ways, yet most people are unwilling to even consider the problem, much less do something about it. Despite the ease with which we talk openly about rape, abortion, homosexuality, wife-swapping, and other previously taboo subjects, incest remains shrouded in silence. Little research has been conducted on incest, and even less has been written about it.

About two years ago, when the idea for this book began to take form, I went to the main branch of the Los Angeles Public Library to see what material on incest was available to the public. In the card catalogue, between 'Inca' and 'Income Tax,' were three books on incest. Two of them were written more than thirty years ago. When I tried to check them out the librarian averted her eyes and asked for my identification. I offered my library card. 'No, no,' she said. 'I mean other identification. A library card isn't enough – those books are about . . .' She looked around conspiratorially, then whispered, '. . . *you* know.' 'Yes,' I replied, '*I* know. I'm the one who wants to check them out.'

After providing my business card and driver's license I was allowed to see the books. They were deadly dull, full of theories that had no practical application either for treating or for understanding incest. I checked too in *Everything You Always Wanted to Know About Sex but Were Afraid to Ask*, by Dr David Reuben, which to me seemed a logical place to look, but there was not even a mention of incest.

Believing deeply that the public must be educated about incest and realizing that no books for general audiences were available I resolved to write this book. I could see no alternative. Through the case histories and analyses in this book, I will point out not only that incest is a pervasive and crushing problem for both individuals and society, but also that incest is not a dead end. I know this from both personal and professional experience.

2 · THE INCEST TABOO

In those few circles where incest is discussed – primarily among psychologists, sociologists, and anthropologists – the act of incest and its effects are rarely mentioned. Instead, conversation centers on the 'incest taboo.' An examination of the taboo (sometimes referred to as the 'horror of incest' or the 'incest dread') is vital to the understanding of human nature, not because it implies a natural aversion to incest, but rather because it implies a natural incest attraction. If we instinctively avoided incestuous behavior, we would have no need to prohibit it. As anthropologist Bronislaw Malinowski wrote in 1926, 'A social taboo does not derive its force from instinct, but instead it always has to work against some innate impulse.' Some innate impulse like incest.

It is only natural for people to become sexually attracted to others with whom they live in close quarters, share meals, and have close emotional ties. However, in our society, a great many social prohibitions are essential for peaceful coexistence, and the incest taboo is one of them. Relationships between family members are complicated and tense enough without sexual competition and jealousy playing a part.

Incestuous desires are in us all, though we engage a variety of unconscious mechanisms to deny them. As infants our sexuality is not focused in our genitals or erogenous zones, it is all over our bodies. Sensuality and sexuality are one to an infant. Every sensation is new and thrilling, whether it be touching a face or being poked in the belly. A drive for sexual pleasure moves us to explore our world, and one of our greatest pleasures is sucking at our mother's breast. Mother, too, derives sexual pleasure from this – this sexuality is nature's safeguard that we will be fed. Thus the act of nursing can be loosely interpreted as an act of incest.

Even if we are bottle-fed, we associate the warmth of being held, the softness of the rubber nipple in our mouth, and the various delights of the warm milk with mother. This is as true for girls as for boys: A child does not really begin to understand sexual differences until he or she is three or four years old. Infants' sexual drives are naturally directed toward their mothers.

When we are separated from mother we miss her tremendously. More and more we realize that much of her time is taken up by father. We learn that she is father's mate, and that there are limitations on the extent of our intimacy with her. We long for her secretly, and we are jealously angry at father for taking her, but we feel guilty about our forbidden thoughts. This guilt is the heart of conscience. We feel incestuously attracted, yet everything we are taught lobbies against that attraction. We are caught in a sexual and emotional Catch-22.

INCEST AND OEDIPUS

The conflict between our incestuous desires and the incest taboo lies at the center of Freud's theory of the Oedipus complex. Though he admitted that female Oedipal development was something of a 'riddle' to him Freud asserted that boys, around age four, want to sexually possess their mothers and replace their fathers (just as Oedipus, in Greek myth, killed his father and married his mother).

I believe Oedipal desires are symbolic emotional desires and indistinct physical urges, rather than specific incestuous scenarios. The very young child does not specifically want to have intercourse with his mother. He wants her undivided attention; he wants to possess her; he wants her to do the things that give him pleasure and that arouse him. If he were older these desires would be sexual urges, but in his infancy and early childhood they are unfocused.

The guilt that eventually stems from these desires creates what Freud called 'Oedipal conflicts.' Whether we are talking about Oedipal conflicts in boys or corresponding conflicts in girls we are talking about conflicts that stem from deeply rooted human desires. There is no escaping it – incestuous desires are at the core of human psychology. Despite the power of these desires the bulk of civilization manages to resist them. That is the doing of the incest taboo.

NEGATIVE MAGIC

Sir James Frazer, in his classic anthropological work, *The Golden Bough*, tried to explain what taboo is by comparing it to sorcery: 'The aim of positive magic or sorcery is to produce a desired event; the aim of negative magic or taboo is to avoid an undesirable one.' If incest went unpunished in the Northern Gilbert Islands, for example, the inhabitants traditionally believed that the sun would fall from the sky. Similar taboo violations on Celebes Island, in Indonesia, were thought to precipitate crop failure, and on Mindanao, in the Philippines, to bring on flooding. Adhering to the taboo was said to prevent these natural disasters.

Taboo is not a simple concept. In our modern society we have a tendency to equate the incest taboo with moral, rather than magical, restrictions. But taboos are not moral issues. For instance, until recently the open discussion of death was taboo in our society, yet there is certainly nothing immoral about such discussion. The true meaning of taboo is difficult for us to pinpoint, for as Freud wrote, 'the concept connoted by [taboo] is one which we no longer possess.' Perhaps the closest we come to it is 'superstition.'

Freud's attempt at defining taboo, in *Totem and Taboo*, is as good as any, though he tells us more about what taboo *isn't* than what it *is*: 'Taboo restrictions are distinct from religious or moral prohibitions. They are not based upon any divine ordinance, but may be said to impose themselves on their own account. They differ from moral prohibitions in that they fall into no system that declares quite generally that certain abstinences must be observed and gives reasons for that necessity. Taboo prohibitions have no grounds and are of unknown origin. Though they are unintelligible to *us*, to those who are dominated by them they are taken as a matter of course.'

In our culture the incest taboo is taken as 'a matter of course.' If asked, the average person would say it would not be proper for a man to marry his mother or sister. But if asked why, he or she probably could come up with no better answer than 'Because it's wrong.'

Incest has probably been 'wrong' since prehistoric times.

THE EVOLUTION OF THE INCEST TABOO

An interesting relationship between the development of the incest taboo throughout history and the development of the taboo in an individual can be described by a jargon-jammed truism of biology: 'Ontogeny recapitulates phylogeny.' This means the development of an individual copies the evolutionary development of the species. Thus a fetus develops its organs in the same order in which those organs evolved over millions of years. The truism also works in psychology. The human race began with an incest impulse – probably hundreds of thousands of years ago – later developed an incest taboo, and taught its members to substitute more appropriate desires for the incestuous ones. Similarly, a child is born with, or quickly develops, an incestuous attraction. Later he learns of the taboo. And still later he learns to divert that attraction to appropriate partners.

There are various theories that attempt to explain how the incest taboo came to evolve, all relating to the customs of ancient cave dwellers. For example, early man dominated his mate by virtue of his greater strength. He considered his 'wife' his property, and he defended her as such. When his sons grew to puberty he protected his wife from their sexual invasion as he defended all his property against them. Eventually this paternally imposed prohibition became a custom, which, in turn, developed into a taboo.

Another theory contends that the taboo grew out of biological necessity. Because ancient humans died at an early age parents were either dead or ravaged by age by the time children reached puberty. The fertile years were short, survival of the species dictated that everyone marry early. Since older siblings would be married by the time younger ones reached puberty siblings rarely married each other. So exogamy – marriage outside the family – became the custom. By the time human life expectancy increased, allowing an age difference between mates, the custom of exogamy had become so entrenched that the incest taboo followed naturally as a means of maintaining the status quo.

Freud suggested that the taboo evolved through a 'primal scene,' a sort of instinctual memory in us all. He envisioned this primal scene as a family in which the sons killed their father to possess their mother, then fought among themselves over her. Eventually they realized they had destroyed the social order and felt remorseful over having committed patricide, so they imposed an incest restriction on themselves as penance. Freud saw the incest taboo as 'the oldest form in which we encounter conscience.'

Many people believe the incest taboo is instinctive, coded in our genes, citing as evidence the universality of the taboo. But, in fact, the taboo is not universal. Many anthropological studies attribute various practices to the taboo, but these practices often stem from different definitions of incest. As nineteenth-century sociologist Emile Durkheim wrote in *Incest: The Nature and Origin of the Taboo*: 'The same cause cannot explain why in one place marriages between maternally related kin are specifically prohibited while elsewhere the prohibition extends to marriages between all consanguine [blood] relatives, why in one society the prohibition reaches out to infinity while in another it does not go beyond the closest collaterals, why among the primitive Hebrews, the ancient Arabs, the Phonoecians, the Greeks, and certain Slavs, did this natural aversion not prevent a man from marrying his father's sister.' Nor is the incest taboo genetic. Witness the Greeks, who within a millennium changed their societal attitude toward incest, yet could not have undergone any significant genetic changes in so short a time.

If primitive societies are any measure, not only is there no one prohibition that can be called an incest taboo, but incest has actually been condoned in one way or another by some cultures. Among the Indians of the Sierra Madre mountains of Mexico father–daughter incest is still common (though sibling incest is almost unknown). This incest is fostered by economics – the Indian works his land fairly far from his home. He must have a woman to grind the corn he picks, so he takes a daughter with him while his wife stays home to run the household and take care of the other children. Because a blanket is a major expenditure he usually has only one, which he shares with his daughter. The combination of physical contact, isolation from others, and custom makes incest virtually unavoidable.

The Kalangs of Java traditionally believe incest with their mothers will ensure prosperity. The tribesmen of Malawi believed intercourse with their sisters would make them bulletproof. Cucis married without regard to blood relationships, with the exception of mothers and sons. Veddahs once thought that marriage to a younger sister was the best possible match, though marriage to an older sister was deplorable. On Bali twins of different sexes, and born into the highest caste, were wed automatically. The people of Taita, in East Africa, often married mothers or sisters for financial reasons – wives outside the family had to be bought. The Ossetes consider it honorable to marry a maternal aunt, but a paternal aunt is out of the question. Among the Yakuts of Siberia it is considered bad luck if a girl's brothers allow her to marry as a virgin, so they take her virginity from her themselves.

William Graham Sumner, in *Folkways, A Study of the Sociological Importance of Usages*, one of the most exhaustive cross-cultural studies of incest ever recorded, concluded, 'The instances show that the notion of incest is by no means universal or uniform, or attended by the same intensity of repugnance. It is not by any means traceable to a constant cause.'

Still, *almost* all societies practice some type of incest prohibition. It must serve some purpose central to human society since almost every culture in history independently developed a form of the taboo. What could that purpose be?

THE PURPOSE OF THE INCEST TABOO – INDEPENDENCE

Throughout nature the major task of parenthood is to prepare the young for independence. Birds teach chicks to fly; lions teach cubs to hunt; humans teach children to speak, to count, to make decisions, to bathe, and all the thousands of other behaviors that are necessary for a human being to function in society after leaving the protection of the home. In no other species is the young animal dependent on its parents for nearly as long as is the human child. The process of preparing a human child for independence is a highly complex one, and the incest taboo does its part to make that process advance as smoothly as possible.

One way the taboo aids this process of personality development is by helping to stabilize the family. Anthropologist A. D. Coult is credited with the theory that the incest prohibition evolved to prevent role confusion within the family. If someone takes on more than one role – like both father and husband to the same person – role strain will result, creating tensions that could destroy the family. Along these lines, psychiatrist Martin Weich developed an interesting theory about the use of the words 'mother,' 'father,' 'sister,' 'brother,' and so on as a defense against incest. By calling family members by their roles, rather than by their given names, we constantly remind ourselves of their roles so we cannot slip into considering them in any other way.

The most critical function of the taboo, however, has to do with socialization, forcing people to seek partners outside the family so that the community will broaden its ties and grow strong. Anthropologist Margaret Mead reported that the Arapesh of Polynesia enforced an incest taboo as a means of socialization. She asked a tribal elder what he thought of a brother and sister marrying. He replied: 'What? You want to marry your sister? Are you not quite right in the head? Don't you want any in-laws? Can't you see that you can gain at least two in-laws if you marry another man's sister and another man marries your sister? With whom will you go hunting and till the fields, and who can you visit?' In our society the needs of socialization are more subtle and complex, but no less important.

Sociologist T. Parsons suggests that not only does the taboo force people to look outside the family for mates, but it also forces them to become psychologically independent of the family, to become individuals. He maintains that this internal socialization is essential to normal character development. The step of breaking away from parents is much easier physically than it is psychologically. The emotional bonds between a child and his or her parents can be difficult and painful to break. The incest taboo prevents the creation of sexual bonds, which would make that break even more difficult.

Sibling incest can also be seen as a threat to independence. There is a great deal of mutual identification between siblings who grow up together. By turning sexually to a sibling, a child avoids the difficult task of breaking out of the family cocoon and establishing an independent identity. The child seeks emotional security in incest.

Those societies and castes throughout history that condoned incest almost always did so to *prevent* socialization. For example, incest has always been most frequently practiced by lines of royalty – like the Incan princes, or the Ptolemies of Egypt – for they wanted to keep the royal blood pure and the royal family insulated from commoners.

INBREEDING

The royal families of Europe suffered from their incestuous practices by perpetuating the family weakness – hemophilia. Inbreeding often results in birth problems. In a 1967 American study, for example, eighteen babies conceived incestuously were compared to eighteen other babies. The mothers had been matched for age, weight, stature, intelligence, and socio-economic status. The incest group showed dramatically more birth defects – five babies died within six months, and only seven were healthy and free of pathology. Only one of the other babies had a serious physical defect, and fifteen were normal and healthy.

Similar results arose from a Czech study of 161 incestuously conceived babies. More than 9 percent of the incest babies died within the first year of life or were stillborn, as opposed to just over 5 percent of the control group. More than 40 percent of the incest babies suffered physical or mental defects, while none of the control group demonstrated any mental deficiencies, and less than 5 percent had physical abnormalities.

On the other hand there are many examples of incest being continued for generations with consistently healthy offspring resulting. The Incan princes kept the bloodline pure by promoting brother–sister marriage through fourteen generations, yet neither their bones nor their extensive written records suggest that the line suffered any physical or mental degeneration. The same is true of the Ptolemies of Egypt, who, after several generations of sibling couplings, produced Cleopatra (whose husband was both her uncle and her brother).

The reason for these genetic successes is that incest does not cause mutations, as is popularly believed. It instead tends to bring out recessive traits in offspring. These are traits – such as hemophilia, diabetes, certain central nervous system diseases, and a variety of harmless traits like certain hair colors – that are coded in the genes but may or may not manifest themselves in offspring, depending on how the genes from both parents mesh. If a certain recessive gene runs in a family, it is likely to pair up with an identical gene in an incestuous union, assuring the manifestation of the recessive trait. Since many negative traits are recessive, incestuous offspring are prone to birth problems. A successful incestuous bloodline, therefore, depends on unusually negative-trait-free recessive genes. As the statistics show, such genes are rare.

Some theorists believe that the incest taboo evolved as a necessary protection against the dangers of inbreeding. I think this is unlikely. It is hard to believe that primitive humans made deductions about breeding across generations from the meager evidence of occasional birth defects. And incest taboos have been recorded in societies that had not yet discovered the relationship between intercourse and pregnancy, much less between inbreeding and birth defects. Clearly, the taboo evolved as a response to more instinctive human motivation.

PITFALLS OF THE TABOO

Some theorists believe the incest taboo does more harm than good. They argue that a great deal of incest trauma is related to a sense of having broken the incest taboo, and to the punishment our society evokes on behalf of that taboo.

According to psychologist R. E. L. Masters, who has written extensively on incest: 'It is easy to show that the severe condemnation of all incestuous unions, and even of incestuous desires, results in great damage to many persons. Unless an immense amount of evidence is to be summarily rejected, we must admit that the incest prohibition is presently functioning to produce all manner of psychosexual and other afflictions.'

There is even a society dedicated to abolishing the incest taboo. Very loosely based on the writings of Rene Guyon, with a gross distortion of Freud added for good measure, the society's slogan is: 'Sex by year eight or else it's too late.' They believe early sex from compassionate adults will reduce violent tendencies in children caused by societal repression. Though the Guyon Society claims a membership of '2000 parents and psychiatrists,' I was unable to find any evidence that the membership exceeds the one person required to print a newsletter.

Most of the serious theorists who question the benefits of the incest taboo do not mean to condone incest, but rather to condemn the traumatic power of the taboo. All too often I've found the taboo to be more effective in preventing the disclosure of incest than in preventing the act itself.

Instead of concentrating on the psychological damage of incest our society tends to focus on the violation of the taboo – causing both victims and aggressors to be too intimidated by the possibility of exposure to seek help. The situation is similar to that faced by alcoholics just a few years ago. Alcoholism often was covered up by the whole family for fear of the shame of discovery. As a result alcoholics drank themselves to death instead of finding treatment.

The incest aggressor who comes forward today can expect little sympathy. We experience the horror of incest, and we react with vengeance. We see him as a monster instead of as a disturbed individual who needs help. This gut-level attitude helps neither the aggressor, the victim, nor the community.

A rational approach to the problem of incest begins with an understanding that, despite the taboo, the roots of incest are in us all, and they are sprouting uncontrollably in our society. Even many of my colleagues in the mental health community have not come to this understanding, believing instead that most incest reports are fantasies.

Too many therapists are still concerned with solving the theoretical mysteries of the taboo instead of dealing with the real incidence of incest. As Lord Raglan wrote in *Incest and Exogamy*, 'The procedure adopted by most of our authorities seems to have been, if I may be allowed the expression, to stare at the incest taboo and scratch their heads.'

I think it's time we stopped scratching and concerned ourselves with the human consequences of the taboo.

3 · THE VICTIM'S ANGUISH

Last year I met a psychiatric nurse whom I considered, after working with her for several months, a competent, intelligent, well-adjusted young woman. One day I mentioned that I was working on this book, and in the course of the ensuing conversation she told me that she had been raped several times by her teenage brother when she was eight, and regularly forced by her father to perform fellatio between the ages of eleven and thirteen. As we talked I began to realize that she was actually severely depressed and disturbed, though she managed to hide her symptoms behind a remarkably solid facade. I asked her how she thought the incest experience had affected her. Her reply still haunts me: 'Think of the lowest thing in the world, and whatever it is, I'm lower.'

That is the motto of the incest victim.

Incest is almost always a devastating experience for the victim. Its emotional and psychological impact is destructive for several reasons – partly because of our cultural reactions to incest, to a greater degree because the child is thrust into an adult role for which he or she is unprepared, and, most tragically, because of the aggressor's betrayal of the child's trust and dependence. The victims are not always innocent in a sexual context, they are not always virginal, but they are generally too young and naïve to understand treachery, and that is the innocence that is so traumatically betrayed in incest. The people they have learned to depend on, trust, and love suddenly turn on them in a bewildering, terrifying, often physically painful fashion.

Incest is powerful. Its devastation is greater than that of nonincestuous child molestation or rape because incest is set within a constellation of family emotions and conflicts. There is no stranger to run from, no home to run to. The child cannot feel safe in his or her own bed. The victim must learn to live with incest; it flavors the child's entire world. The aggressor is always there, incest is often a continuing horror for the victim.

Few studies that have been conducted agree on the average duration of incestuous relationships. In a classic study of two hundred Chicago cases conducted by Weinberg in the early 1960s, 74 percent of the relationships were found to have lasted less than one year, while only 13 percent lasted more than three years. On the other hand German researcher Herbert Maisch reported in 1972 that 71 percent of the fifteen hundred cases he studied went on for more than a year, with the average length being three years. I have seen cases ranging from five minutes to eighteen years, but I've found no correlation between the duration of an incestuous relationship and the type or amount of damage done to the victim.

Various studies have found the average age of the incest victim to be from eleven to thirteen years – around puberty – but in my own practice the average seems younger, around seven or eight. I have seen cases in which incestuous contact began when the child was less than two years old, and a colleague once told me of a case of a seven-day-old infant who was so badly molested that she required hospitalization. Though some experts claim that prepubescent victims experience less trauma than adolescent victims – presumably because a young child is less likely to blame him- or herself for the incest – this theory has not proved out in my practice. As with the duration of incestuous relationships I have found no pattern tying a victim's age to the type or measure of trauma suffered.

An understanding of incest will not be derived from statistics, but rather from the experiences of incest participants. In this chapter I will focus on the feelings and behavior of female victims, since almost 90 percent of all incest victims are female. But the dynamics I will describe – the emotional geography of incest – are generally applicable to male victims as well.

RECURRING THEMES

Certain themes emerge from the incest experiences of almost every victim – a craving for love from the aggressor; little resistance to incestuous advances; in some cases enjoyment of incestuous sex, in some cases, repulsion; stressful secrecy about the incest; and tremendous guilt.

Most victims feel unloved by other family members, and will go to almost any lengths to reverse that feeling. The victim craves the love of her father or her brother, and often feels a normal sexual attraction for them. She is set up, by her own emotional needs, to be sexually abused.

When a father makes incestuous advances toward his daughter, he rarely resorts to force or violence – he has no need. There is a tremendous psychological coercion built into the father–daughter relationship. Not only has the daughter been taught to obey her father, but she looks to him for moral guidance. If daddy says it is all right, it must be. Then, of course, if she considers disobeying her father, the threat of punishment is always hanging in the air. So the victim almost always participates in the incest 'voluntarily,' not recognizing the subtle coercion that has taken place.

Often the victim will enjoy incestuous caresses – they may represent the only affection she has ever known. She may experience physical pleasure from her father's ministrations, and she senses that she gives him pleasure. He treats her as if she were special, and she loves the attention.

Just as often, however, the victim experiences pain, fear, and revulsion. Vaginal penetration can cause physical as well as psychological damage to a young girl. Oral sex often nauseates victims. Even manual stimulation can be painful. The victim is also usually aware of the taboo to some extent, and she feels that what she is doing is 'dirty.'

The victim may be afraid of being beaten, removed from the home, or disbelieved, so she usually tells no one about the incest. Her shame seals her silence. Sometimes she fears that her father will be put in jail if she informs on him, and there will be no one to provide for the family. Or she may remain silent for fear of self-incrimination. For whatever reason the victim is drawn into a world of secrecy – a world of shame, hopelessness, and guilt – where she feels isolated from everyone else. There is no one to turn to, no one to confide in, no one to ask for help. The young, vulnerable, inexperienced child must cope by herself in a cold, unsupportive family environment with the explosive conflicts and the guilt generated by incest.

Amid her craving for love, her seemingly voluntary involvement in the incest, her possible enjoyment of it, and her complicity in the cover-up, the victim comes away from incest with overwhelming feelings of responsibility and guilt.

RECURRING SYMPTOMS

As the victim grows older her guilt often makes her self-destructive – she punishes herself for the 'sin' she imagines herself to have committed. She suffers fundamental lack of self-confidence and self-respect; she feels undeserving of emotional, physical, or material satisfaction.

She has feelings of betrayal and self-loathing. Because her first experiment with trust was such a painful failure, she cannot bring herself to trust again. Her distrust alone is enough to ensure that she will not allow herself to become close to a man. And her self-loathing tends to project itself as hostility, so she also has trouble making friends with women.

If as a child she found the incest painful or frightening, after puberty she may perceive sex as a symbolic replay of the incest and be revolted by it. She may have originally protected herself from the pain and ugly reality of incestuous penetration by blocking out all genital sensations. Later the repression of her sexual feelings easily becomes habitual. Still, even though she derives no pleasure from sex, her need for self-punishment as a response to her guilt may drive her to have sex with a variety of men. She may be promiscuous as a means of self-degradation, while at the same time seeking through sex the affection she never quite found in incest. Because she confuses love, guilt, and sex, she ends up too often being used as a sexual object.

Through her continual self-punishment she tries to cleanse herself of guilt, but her feelings won't wash away. Since she cannot punish herself sufficiently she may seek a mate to do it for her. Because of this tendency many victims become 'incest carriers.' Because they marry men who are likely to be irresponsible, have poor impulse control, and have little respect for other people – prime candidates to become aggressors – their children often become victims.

The victim may often manifest her guilt in psychosomatic symptoms – most often migraines. Any of the symptoms often associated with tension may appear, including stomach ailments, skin disorders, and disabling aches and pains. Though not every victim I have seen has suffered all of these symptoms, I have yet to see a victim who does not suffer from a combination of several of them. It is hardly surprising that most victims experience periods of deep depression, often leading to attempted suicide.

THE SOCIAL IMPACT OF INCEST

The incest victim's need for self-punishment often leads her into self-abusive behaviors like alcoholism, drug abuse, or prostitution. Since various studies place the percentage of incest victims in the general population between 3 and 30 percent – I estimate the number to be somewhere between ten and twenty million Americans – these antisocial behaviors add up to a significant social problem.

In those segments of our society where self-destructive and antisocial behavior is commonplace – among drug addicts, for example – incest victims are heavily represented. Odyssey House, a residential drug treatment program with centers throughout the country, reports that 44 percent of its female drug addicts had been incestuously abused as children. John Siverson, a Minneapolis therapist who has treated over five hundred teenage drug addicts, reportedly estimates that figure to be closer to 70 percent.

A study of 150 rapists in New Jersey found that 75 percent of them had been sexually abused as children.

Studies of prostitutes have also yielded high incidence of incest. Jennifer James, of the University of Washington in Seattle, found that of two hundred prostitutes interviewed, one out of four had been a victim of incest. Other studies have placed the figure closer to 75 percent.

Adolescent victims often become runaways. Researchers at Odyssey House found that more than half of the female incest victims in their study had left home before their seventeenth birthday. Twenty-three percent had run away by age fourteen. The possibility of incest is too often ignored by police and juvenile authorities in runaway cases – the runaway is often treated as a criminal when she is actually taking positive action to solve a serious problem. But usually a runaway victim is returned to her parents without being questioned about why she ran away in the first place. Thus the incest is blindly perpetuated.

An adolescent incest victim has four choices: She can put up with the sexual abuse; she can escape through drugs, alcohol, or psychological breakdown; she can inform authorities and perhaps take responsibility for imprisoning her father and impoverishing her family (if anyone believes her, that is); or she can run away. Given those choices running away is neither delinquent nor even immature – it is a logical response to a desperate situation.

INFORMING – A VARIETY OF NIGHTMARES

Police departments across the country are beginning to gain a sensitivity to the problem of incest, but the problem is complex, and police education will take some time. I sometimes consult with police departments on the handling of incest cases, and when I raise the question of runaways, I am invariably asked why these children don't turn to the other parent, another relative, or a teacher. Unfortunately, there are several reasons.

If the child had a close enough relationship with the other parent to confide such a 'shameful' secret, chances are the incest would not have occurred in the first place. Incest usually *follows* a breakdown in family communications. Also, in many cases the child may perceive her mother as a participant in the incest (I will discuss the mother's participation in Chapter Five), and sees no advantage in informing her of it.

The victim may also fear breaking up the family or disrupting her own life. She may believe that disclosure of the incest will lead to her being placed in a foster home – which, in fact, often occurs. This happened to one of my patients who was raped by her older brother when she was twelve. When she informed the authorities she, not her brother, was placed outside the home. She perceived this action as a form of punishment, and it has complicated her treatment considerably. It is difficult to persuade someone that she holds no responsibility for an act when she considers herself imprisoned for it.

Many victims do not inform on the aggressor because they enjoy the incestuous contact. Even if the incest is discovered these victims will often refuse to testify against the aggressor, for they may experience the sexuality of incest as a measure of love, and would consider any action against the aggressor a betrayal of that love.

Victims who *do* inform may run into a variety of problems. The legal process can be painful and humiliating for an incest victim. She may be required to relive the experience before a courtroom of strangers more than once, and she may be mercilessly cross-examined by the aggressor's attorney. If the aggressor denies his involvement, the victim may not be believed, or she may be persuaded by her mother or her attorney to recant her accusation.

If the aggressor is convicted, the victim's mother typically blames her for resultant financial and emotional hardships, making family life miserable for the victim.

But the most tragic reaction to a victim's admission or accusation is a repetition of the incest betrayal. This is especially common when the victim informs other relatives – grandparents, uncles, cousins, etc. The best way to describe this repeated betrayal is to present an example.

Nicole James

Nicole James was raised in an upper-middle-class suburb of Minneapolis. Her father was the manager of a foundry. Her mother, later described in Nicole's psychiatric records as an 'ambulatory psychotic,' was a large woman who regularly beat her five children, of which Nicole was the youngest.

I first met Nicole when she was twenty-three. She had swallowed about three hundred pills of various types, and had drunk a fifth of Scotch – in her sixth suicide attempt.

By the time she entered one of my inpatient groups she had been interviewed by two psychiatrists, but she had refused to talk about her suicide attempt. I remember first seeing her and thinking how vacant her heart-shaped face appeared. She was slightly chubby, with curly brown hair and large brown eyes. As I spoke with her I understood what the referring psychiatrist had meant when he remarked, 'She has an inner emptiness that is chilling.'

It took several weeks of therapy before she came to trust me and the rest of the group, but one day, after another patient shared an incest experience, Nicole found the courage to tell her own.

'All I remember,' she said, 'is going upstairs in the bedroom and both of my brothers approaching me. I was six years old. One brother was twelve, the other seven. My older brother had intercourse with me. I can't remember whether the seven-year-old did anything or not. This continued on and off from then until I was thirteen, with both brothers, but mainly the older one.

'I never told my parents because, after it first happened, my brothers told my parents that I had my clothes off, so my father beat the hell out of me. After that I never told them anything.

'I thought what was happening was *maybe* normal, but I still felt something funny was going on. I didn't know what it was. I knew it wasn't right; even when I was a child – eight or nine years old – I knew something was wrong, but I couldn't define it.'

As Nicole grew older and began to understand what her brothers were doing to her she sought help from an uncle.

'My uncle told me – I think I was about fourteen – that he was going to show me that men weren't all bad, so he started in on me when my brothers stopped. This went on until I was seventeen. There was oral sex and, to put it bluntly, jacking him off, and rectal sex. There was never any intercourse with my uncle though. He told me he respected me too much for that.

'I didn't think I had any choice. I felt it was my duty. His wife was crippled and I guess she didn't satisfy him. I was afraid to stop. Finally I tried to escape by the only way I could think of – suicide.'

In the five years since then Nicole has made five more suicide attempts. Her psychiatric record reads like a textbook on depression. She suffers from severe leg and back pains which she explains as 'paying for my sins.'

Since her incest has come out into the open where she can work with it she has finally begun to show signs of improvement. Her physical symptoms are beginning to recede, and her periods of depression are becoming shorter and less severe. She still has quite a job before her, though, if she is to recover to the point of being able to lead a normal life.

Nicole's story is not unique. I have heard similar stories repeatedly from my patients, and similar accounts have been reported by other therapists. Dr Roland Summit and JoAnn Kryso, M. S. W., consultants in the field of sexual abuse of children, wrote recently that a victim 'may be regarded by relatives as dangerously attractive ... Publicly deflowered as she is, she is regarded as no longer deserving of respect or protection. We know of at least four cases where male relatives have attempted seduction after a girl has admitted incest with her father.'

This loss of bodily privacy and respect will crop up in case histories throughout this book. Victims who admit to incest, or who are discovered, are often called liars or sluts. Unfortunately they come to believe these denunciations.

DEALING WITH THE MEMORY OF INCEST

All incest victims could use help and understanding, no matter how successfully they seem to function. The incest trauma can smolder in a victim's unconscious and cause symptoms for a lifetime if it is not treated. Some victims are able to function without therapy, some are not. Those who cope appear to have successfully overcome their emotional and psychological reaction to incest. But most of these victims have merely resigned themselves to their symptoms, and may be far from healthy.

Those victims unable to cope are usually pushed into therapy by either psychological or legal pressures. They are the lucky ones, for they receive help.

I estimate that 20 percent of all the psychiatric patients I see were once victims of incest. I am not talking about patients who are referred to me because of my expertise in incest, I am talking about the general populations of the various psychiatric hospitals in which I work. Twenty percent! And for every victim who seeks treatment there are probably ten who do not – millions of hurting people who apparently don't know they can be helped.

4 · THE AGGRESSOR'S BITTER VICTORY

There is a tribe in South Africa, along the Nkotami River, that once specialized in hunting hippopotami. Incest was strictly forbidden in this tribe. When a hunter was ready to embark on a month-long hunt he spent a day ostensively fishing, but actually spying on the hippopotami, watching their every move. When he felt sufficiently prepared he called his daughter to his hut and had sexual relations with her. This made him a murderer, for he had killed something within himself by committing incest. As a murderer he had the courage to kill a hippopotamus, and so, that very night, he moved onto the river. Only after he had killed his hippopotamus was his honor restored.

Stripped of its symbolic trappings this ritual points out an inevitable result of incest – the aggressor, too, suffers. Something inside him dies. Like the Nkotami hunter the Western aggressor commits incest to fulfill an internal need. But when he navigates the river of his consciousness he finds no victory to ameliorate his guilt.

To portray him most clearly I will narrow my scope to one type of aggressor in this chapter. Since three out of every four reported cases involve father–daughter incest I will concentrate on the incestuous father. But the dynamics I will discuss are generally applicable to most types of aggressors.

WHO IS THE INCESTUOUS FATHER?

The incestuous father is the most misunderstood sex criminal in our society – and the easiest to rehabilitate. He is rarely a freak, a dangerous criminal, or a psychotic. Instead, he is often an otherwise law-abiding, hard-working guy-next-door who, somewhere along the line, has lost the ability to control his impulses. This loss is the crux of his problem, for incestuous desires, as discussed in Chapter Two, occur in everyone. It is his acting on those desires that sets the incestuous father apart. No one really knows what robs him of his self-control, but it is not necessarily a lack of 'moral fiber,' as many people assume. Incestuous fathers are often baffled and horrified at their own behavior.

Most of us manage to develop psychological safeguards against our incestuous desires. In fact, these safeguards are usually so strong that we may not even recognize the existence of our incestuous desires. Incestuous fathers hit a snag somewhere in the development of these safeguards. The temptation of incest brings out the Mr Hyde in them. They are not, however, 'crazy.' The German psychologist Ebber concluded in 1937, after intensive case studies, that 'it is not the mentally sick type, nor the weak-witted, nor the hyper-sexual or sexually abnormal man, nor the man with the most inferior character who is dominant amongst those committing incest.' Maisch came to the same conclusion, calling his fifteen hundred cases 'a completely heterogeneous picture.'

There are, however, certain traits that stand out in this 'heterogeneous picture.' For example I have noticed that most of the incest aggressors I treat tend to be relatively intelligent men. The Kinsey study bears out this observation. Comparing convicted incest aggressors with various other imprisoned, sexually delinquent groups – rapists, child molesters, exhibitionists, etc. – the study found that incest aggressors were the most intelligent.

Incestuous fathers have often been either physically or emotionally abused as children. They often characterize their brothers and sisters as having been favored by their parents. These aggressors typically recall severe beatings by their fathers, and describe their mothers as distant, unapproachable, and sometimes hostile. Incestuous fathers have rarely had an opportunity to learn what constitutes healthy family life.

Ironically many aggressors are regular churchgoers. Their religious beliefs frequently contribute to their incestuous motivations by preventing them from going outside their marriage to meet unfulfilled needs. One Catholic aggressor, when asked by the police why he had seduced his daughter instead of having an affair or hiring a prostitute, replied incredulously, 'What? And cheat on my wife?' Indeed Catholics – whose religious training relies heavily on the exploitation of parishioners' guilt –

constitute a disproportionately large percentage of incest aggressors and victims (44 percent of the Odyssey House study).

Aside from these few generalities not much can be said about the type of person who resorts to incest. He could be anyone. Despite how little we know about who the aggressor is, however, we do know quite a lot about why he commits incest.

THE INCESTUOUS FATHER'S MOTIVATIONS

Aggressors rarely commit incest to satisfy purely sexual needs. Instead they use sex with their young daughters as a vain attempt to satisfy a variety of emotional needs – needs they are not able to understand, that they have no way of knowing how to meet appropriately. Sometimes, to defend against deep feelings of inadequacy, a father commits incest as an exercise of power, a demonstration of the strength that is often frustrated outside the home. In most cases, however, incest is the aggressor's attempt to find the tenderness and understanding that should issue from his relationship with his wife but usually does not. At the same time – whether he pursues power or love – he may be unconsciously seeking revenge against either his wife or his mother for what he considers a variety of emotional crimes against him.

Those aggressors who pursue power through incest are often violent men. They are frequently unable to keep a job, maintain friendships, or escape a domineering parent. They assert their manhood by tyrannizing their families. Physical threats or abuse are the only tools by which they can persuade themselves of their potency.

Despite this tendency toward violence such an aggressor rarely resorts to violence when initiating incest. There is no need. To him sex and violence are equivalent means to the same end – power. If he can demonstrate that power sexually, he has no need for violence. In fact fewer than 1 percent of my patients report being violently molested (though they often recall *threats* of violence to ensure secrecy). Most often the aggressor's authority-figure role is powerful enough to cause a child to submit to sexual abuse. If not he uses whatever force is necessary to ensure the victim's cooperation.

These aggressors are often alcoholics. Various studies show that anywhere from 20 to 30 percent of all incest cases involve alcohol; I would estimate that in cases of tyrannical fathers the figure is closer to 50 percent. They often turn to alcohol for the same reason they turn to incest – as a method of coping with their feelings of inadequacy. It is invariably an unsuccessful method.

The more common type of aggressor is nonviolent. He turns to incest as a response to loneliness and emotional neglect. Although he may be a good father in every other respect, he loses control at some point and is virtually victimized by his own impulses. This does not alleviate his responsibility for the incest, but his actions are generally less malicious than those of the violent aggressor. If his daughter resists his advances he may resort to blackmail. For example, one of my patients was a woman whose parents were both blind. Her father forced her to have intercourse with him from the time she was five until she was eight. By the time she got to me, twenty-five years later, she had survived five suicide attempts and was nearly psychotic. I asked her why she had allowed her father to catch her. Surely if he was blind she could have escaped his advances. She said, 'He told me he wouldn't give me any food or clothes if I didn't do what he wanted. I thought he would toss me out in the street.'

Another of my patients had been having intercourse with her father from puberty until she married at eighteen. After her wedding she assumed that her involvement with her father was over. He felt differently, however, and resorted to blackmail. He threatened to tell her husband about the incestuous relationship if she didn't continue to 'service' him. She was afraid her husband would find her repulsive if he discovered the incest, so she submitted to her father's demands. Eventually she entered one of my outpatient groups on the verge of a breakdown. In treatment we worked out a way for her to confess the relationship to her husband. Her father, robbed of his ammunition, was not only rejected, but exposed. His response was to blame the victim for seducing him (an accusation that her husband, luckily, did not believe).

I have yet to meet an aggressor who openly understands and admits his responsibility for the incest. The reaction is classic – denial of guilt and projection of blame onto the victim or his own wife. Even when he admits to having been the seducer he rarely believes that the responsibility was his alone. This attitude defines the character of the case we are about to examine.

Daniel Alman

I first met Daniel Alman when I was doing consultant work for the center in which he is receiving treatment. Because of his quiet charm and gentleness many of the female staff members had become extremely protective and mothering toward him. They had come to share his belief that his wife was responsible for his problems because of her emotional neglect. I pointed out to them that no matter how rejecting a wife may be, no matter how seductive children may be, the adult aggressor is the only participant who is always in a position to stop or prevent incest, and so the responsibility is *always* his.

Daniel is a handsome man, thirty-one years old, with silky brown hair and brown eyes. He is small, but solidly built. He speaks almost in a whisper.

Daniel was born in Houstan, Texas. His parents were divorced when he was a year old. He has few memories of his father: 'He beat me for crying. I remember being scared to death of my father. That's one of the reasons my mother left him. I'd cry at night and he'd get up and beat me until I was black and blue.'

Daniel lived with his mother and his older sister. Two years later his mother remarried, and two stepbrothers joined the family. His stepfather was a pipeline worker for an oil company, and his mother was a housewife. He remembers little but discord in the family – conflicts usually split along bloodlines.

'I remember fighting everybody all the time,' he recalls. 'By the time I got into seventh grade it wasn't that I was trying to be bad, it was more like self-defense – a means of survival. I was small, and we were poor. Someone would make a remark about the holes in your clothes, you know, so you go over and punch him out. I was in with a crowd that just got drunk, fought, and chased girls – that's all there was to life.

'At home life was miserable. My parents were very, very strict Protestants. We went to church four times a week. You just didn't go anywhere except church. My stepfather was very strict about that, and he'd whip you if you were bad. His favorite method was to get a branch off a tree and use it on bare legs. He would draw blood and raise welts. The whole family was pretty tense.

'When I was nineteen I got drafted. I went into the navy and was shipped to Vietnam. I worked as an electronics technician doing radio installations in the war zone. When I came back I think I was a lot older and a lot wiser. Just getting away from all the drinking and fighting at home was enough.

'I went to work and started seeing women. I can't remember ever in my life being without at least a casual girlfriend. Soon after I came back from the service I met my first wife. She was beautiful, sort of strawberry blonde, blue eyes – a Swede with that really nice complexion that so many of them have. While we were going together she got pregnant. We probably should have gotten married at that time, but I refused to just because she got pregnant. It wasn't so much that I didn't want to, but I didn't like being forced into anything. So she had the baby and put it up for adoption. It was a boy. I don't think I've ever quite gotten over that. If I sat here and thought about it a few minutes I would probably start crying about it.

'Six months later I started thinking about what had really happened – he was my child and now he's gone. That's when it really started getting to me. That's when we decided to get married. I'm sure my wife resented the fact that I hadn't married her before. As a matter of fact she refused to have any more children, and I think that's part of the reason I left her two years later. We had a very even relationship, never fought.

'While we were married I went back to college to get my degree in accounting. That's where I met Sandy, who eventually became my second wife. She had been married and had two daughters, but the marriage had broken up. We started having lunch together and eventually we ended up in bed.

'I felt really bad about that because I was still married. It made me feel guilty to go home and sleep with my wife because I knew that when I was with her I was thinking that I wanted to be with Sandy. I left my wife about a month later.

'When I moved in with Sandy her girls were four and two. They're both beautiful kids, blonde hair, blue eyes. Sandy has dark hair that she either streaks or dyes blonde, and she's got brownish eyes. She's only about four-eleven, a hundred and ten pounds. She's very small.

'She and I felt very close. We would talk to each other and feel free to discuss almost anything. And then she got pregnant.

'That pregnancy seemed to change the relationship quite a bit. Sandy sort of isolated herself from me. She didn't want to share any of her feelings and when she did she was usually very hostile, very negative. She blamed me because she got pregnant, but she also blamed herself.

'She didn't want the baby. When she got pregnant she just turned off to me. Even before she got pregnant she would withdraw sometimes, not want to have sex for maybe two weeks. But after she got pregnant it got really bad. And when she changed it started changing me. I was seeing something that meant so much to me getting away and I didn't have any control over it whatsoever. I just kept wondering what in the hell was going on. I was trying to get her to tell me what she was feeling so I could do something, and she just wouldn't. It was just, "Get the hell away from me; I don't feel good; don't touch me; don't talk to me; just leave me alone."

'At that time I was working as an accountant, and I had worked my way up to a relatively high position, but I was working eighty hours a week to do it and Sandy complained that I didn't spend enough time at home. I was under a lot of pressure at the job and a lot of pressure at home, and I just couldn't seem to please everybody. I wanted to be home more, but when I got there I felt like I wasn't home. A lot of times she'd start a fight as soon as I walked in the door. Or she just wouldn't say anything and that would be worse.

'Eventually I quit that job and started doing landscaping. I was working with my hands, working outside, a lot less pressure, and I was home a lot more. She was happy about that, but by that time things had gotten so bad that it was very difficult to talk to her. I couldn't say anything to her without her getting hostile.

'About three months after I quit the accounting job things started happening with the girls. They were four and six. I can't really pinpoint when it started. I used to walk around in my shorts in the morning, and the girls would be in their pajamas or whatever – my wife would be asleep – and we would horse around, just playing. They would try to pull my shorts down or something like that. I didn't think anything of it, they'd seen me naked before.

'But as time wore on it would be them trying to touch me or actually touching me – I don't know if you'd call it in a sexual way, but in a way that could be sexually arousing. I told them not to do that. I didn't want to panic them by telling them that's terrible, but I told them not to do it. But they thought it was a game. And maybe subconsciously I didn't want them to stop and didn't make it clear enough. In a way I might have been giving them a double message – stop, but don't. But each time anything happened it got worse and worse.

'My wife was working at night, and wouldn't get home a lot of times until midnight, so I would have to get the kids dinner and put them to bed and all that. The older one would come up to me and say, "Would you take your pants down?" and I would say no. Then she would go through her routine of, you know, "Aw, come on, please," and at times she would even start crying. Most of the time I would just have to run into the other room or get rough enough with her that I felt bad. But sometimes things just led to other things, and pretty soon we would be involved in oral sex.

'The girls would take turns. The older one would ask me if she could, well, lick my penis, and the younger one would just do it because the older one did. But I would start to realize what was going on, and just panic. I'd lose my erection – I never ejaculated with them – and have to get away. The older one would say, "Would you kiss me here?" and touch herself on the vagina. I don't think she had any orgasmic feelings, but I know she was enjoying it. She said it felt good. She seemed to demand it more as it went along. To the younger one it was just a game.

'When it would happen I don't think I thought about much of anything. It's like a part of me would just go away. I would be somebody else. It was like I was watching somebody else from a very distant place. I can't say that I felt sexual. Initially I would start by feeling very close to the children, but then everything would start to shut down. Like there wasn't any physical feeling involved. In a way it was like dreaming. Things are happening and you're not really there.

'After it was over I would feel very guilty and then I would just stop thinking about it, period. I can remember going into the bedroom and just wanting to scream. I probably did a couple of times. I asked myself, "Why is this happening?" It was something I wasn't looking for, and all of a sudden it was there.

'Sometimes I would push the girls away – tell them "Get away from me." But sometimes I would initiate things. Just having them close to me could start things up. I'd felt close to them before and they hadn't brought out this type of reaction, but all of a sudden ... it scared the hell out of me. I can't remember ever being afraid of anything else to the point of panic, but this did it.

'They asked me if they could tell their mother, and I told them not to because it would hurt her a lot. So they said okay. They just seemed to accept it. They knew it was wrong, because I had told them. I sat down and told them it's not right to do this – "We're not going to do it anymore." But it must not have been a strong enough order.

'They were going to a therapist during this whole thing because their mother thought they might have problems adjusting to her divorce. The oldest one seemed to be handling it all right, but the little one seemed to have a great deal of hostility and difficulty relating to people. So they went to a psychiatric clinic for children, and during one of their sessions, the incest came out. August the 12th, to be exact. The therapist called the police and they tried to talk my wife into putting me in prison. When she refused they threatened to take the kids away from her.

'I got home that day and no one was there. I figured she'd taken the kids out shopping or something. About eight she got home and just walked in and said, "I have to talk to you about something." I could tell by the look in her eyes that it was going to be something big. I didn't know what it was, though, at least not consciously. She started out with, "You know I'm taking the girls to therapy," and the more she talked the closer she got. By the time she told me she had taken the girls away I knew what she was going to say. She was angry to the point of being very cold – icy fury. If she had had a gun she'd have probably shot me.

'I can't say that I remember how I felt – numb, I guess. Guilty, of course. Anger at myself. Wanting desperately for her to understand. I knew she was going to leave me. I was afraid of that.

'I felt like I had to kill myself, because that's probably what I would have done to someone else if he had done the same things I had. I don't know. I spent all that night without really thinking anything that was very rational. I remember my wife calling me from time to time. She had calmed down quite a bit and was worried about me.

'I guess my wife still cares, because she won't prosecute, but chances of reconciliation are just about zero. She doesn't feel she can trust me. She is sure that the kids have been emotionally damaged by what happened, and she makes damned sure that I know it. She has spent hours telling me how much she hates me, and that the children will never be the same. I listen to her because I hope that she can get enough hate and hostility out, if not to enable us to get back together, at least to enable her to get to the point where she can have a normal relationship with somebody else. I was the one person she trusted.

'I started therapy about three days after the whole thing blew up, but the night before I went in, I stuck a shotgun in my mouth and pulled the trigger. The ammunition was about ten years old, apparently too old to go off. There are times now when I still get the urge.

'I think it will be quite a while before I see other women. I have some friends, but I don't care to be around them much. I'm just doing all I can to bring my family back together. Sandy and I are going to joint counseling, though at first she refused. Just absolutely refused. She's been vacillating back and forth from intense hatred to wanting to be with me. Sometimes she'll even come over and spend the night. I don't think Sandy will ever reconcile with me, but as long as there's even a chance in a million, I'm going to try. I love her and I love the girls. She's the only wife I want and they're the only family I want.

'I know it wouldn't happen again if we got together, because I would make sure I knew myself. Knew what was happening to me. There was a time there when I was so confused emotionally that I didn't understand what was happening, what I needed. I didn't know anything. After all that's happened I can't see being in that frame of mind again.'

Daniel illustrates perfectly the complexity of incest motives. He never had a stable homelife as a child, so he came to cherish the dream of a 'happy family' with almost religious fervor. His mother married a violent man whom Daniel grew to hate, and who divided the home into opposing camps. Daniel felt isolated and abandoned by his mother.

The vast majority of aggressors come from what the Kinsey study characterized as 'relatively miserable' family situations. The mother is often absent physically or, as in Daniel's case, emotionally. The absence of a boy's first love-object is felt as a powerful rejection. He grows up insecure, resentful, and fearful of women — fearful of being hurt once again. These feelings are easily transferred to wives and daughters.

On the other hand a boy's Oedipal attraction for his mother is easily transferred to his daughter. Psychoanalyst Ernest Jones concluded as early as 1938 that 'a man who displays an abnormally strong affection for his daughter also has a strong fixation on his mother.'

Daniel was trying to escape his love-hate conflict over his mother by immersing himself in his happy family, but when Sandy became pregnant and began to withdraw he experienced a replay of his mother's rejection. Then, when his stepdaughters became seductive, he experienced a replay of his Oedipal fantasies.

Daniel did not have the control to reject the girls' sexual advances. He thought he could put an end to the sexual play gently, but he could not. His own needs were too strong and too complex. He was afraid of losing the girls' affection, and that affection was the only love he felt was left in the family. In essence he participated in the incest because of his need *to keep the family together*.

The concept of incest as a strategy to keep the family together may be difficult to accept, but I've seen it in case after case. A team of Marine Corps physicians concluded from a 1966 six-case study that incest served 'to reduce family tension by preventing confrontation with the sources of tension. The preservation of the family group is the central function of incest to the group.'

To Daniel the family was everything. He was not looking for sex with his daughters, he was looking for love. But his wife's sexual rejection hit him hard. He might have sought an affair or a prostitute, but his memories of the guilt that had followed his previous adultery prevented him from going outside his marriage. When he was confronted with sexual arousal from the girls his sexual frustration made the temptation more difficult to reject. Daniel was caught in the midst of a typical incest setting – unresolved conflicts about his parents, his wife's sexual and emotional abandonment of him, their inability to talk out their problems, and the innocent play with the girls that evolved into sexuality. He wanted nothing more than to hold his family together, but he felt it coming apart. He was desperate and confused, and in that state of mind he lost control.

After the incest was discovered Daniel was hit with the realization that he had, in fact, destroyed the very family he wanted so badly. Despite his denial of ultimate responsibility he felt guilty over having ruined not only his own life, but that of his wife, whom he suspects will never be able to trust a man again, and the lives of the girls, whom his wife assures him will never recover from the experience. The pressure from this guilt led him to attempt suicide, which, by chance, was unsuccessful. There is no guarantee that he will not try again. Though his therapy seems to be going well he has yet to accept his full responsibility for the incest. That is the first and inescapable step on the road to rehabilitation.

If we are to deal with incest as a social problem we must realize that aggressors differ from the rest of us only insofar as they are unable to control very normal impulses. The majority of incestuous fathers respond well to treatment and many have been successfully reunited with their families. Though there are some men whose violent or sadistic impulses are so deeply ingrained that both their families and society are better served by their imprisonment, they are not common. Viewing incest aggressors as human beings may be our hardest task in understanding and reducing incest in our society – especially by the millions who have been victimized by such men – but it is a necessary step. We cannot restore Dr Jekyll by slaying Mr Hyde.

5 · THE SILENT PARTNER

The most enigmatic figure in the father–daughter incest drama is the mother. Some psychologists insist that she is a participant whether she knows about the incest or not, though her participation is often characterized more by what she does *not* do than by what she does. These theorists believe that mothers of victims are aware either consciously or unconsciously of the incest, or contribute to the incest by neglecting their husbands or by pushing their daughters into the maternal role. I strongly disagree that *all* mothers participate in or know of incest when it occurs – I have worked with mothers who I am convinced were completely innocent of any involvement. But such innocence can only be attributed to a minority.

In this chapter I will discuss those mothers who *are* involved in the incest. They probably account for 80 to 90 percent of all victims' mothers. Of these participating mothers, according to the Kinsey study of sex offenders, only 6 percent are actively, consciously involved. The more typical victim's mother participates in the incest on an unconscious level. She is the silent partner.

In examining both the silent partner and the actively involved mother I will divide their participation into two distinct categories – activity leading up to the incest and activity in response to the discovery of it.

THE SILENT PARTNER

There is a broad spectrum within which the silent partner's unconscious involvement can fall, ranging from ignoring signs that incest is going on to subtly promoting it. Such a mother is often unaware, even after the incest has come to light, that she has played a part in it, but in truth her role is often pivotal.

Typically the silent partner is unable to maintain any sort of nurturing, affectionate relationship with either her husband or her daughter. This emotional abandonment of the family often causes the husband and the daughter to seek emotional refuge with each other. As one of my patients once said: 'We were all starved in my family – not for food, we always had plenty of money – but for feelings. Nobody ever seemed to feel anything. At least when I had sex with my father I could feel *something*.'

The silent partner often pulls back from her family in an attempt to discard her emotional duties. She is often disappointed and bored with her husband, and feels that her marriage is more a habit than anything else. She may feel depressed at the realization that she is no longer as young and attractive as she used to be, and she may envy or resent her daughter's youth and burgeoning sexuality. Her dreams of marital bliss are dissolving around her. Disenchantment is her constant companion. Finding no fulfillment at home she may turn her attention elsewhere, developing new interests – volunteer work, school, a job, social commitments – as a means of escape.

The silent partner's general disenchantment – and resultant emotional neglect of her family – is subtle, not very different from the general disenchantment that seems to be afflicting great numbers of married women these days. What sets the silent partner apart is her tendency to deal with her problems by passing them along to her daughter. She unconsciously abdicates her maternal role in a gradual transfer of duties that have become unpleasant to her, ranging from housekeeping to sex.

This process is sometimes greatly accelerated if the silent partner has severe physical or emotional problems that make her unable to fulfill her maternal role. Once the maternal mantle is partly passed on the remainder of the transfer – the sexual duties – frequently follows.

When a sexual transfer of roles occurs, even if the mother had no conscious intention of promoting such a transfer, the victim often feels as betrayed by her mother's failure to have recognized and stopped the incest as she does by her father's sexual abuse. I run into this continually in therapy. When victims are given an opportunity to vent their feelings toward their mothers they invariably become enraged, as the following case illustrates.

Jane Fowler

Jane Fowler is a tall, handsome black woman who entered the hospital because she felt stressed to the point of being afraid that she would harm her own children. When she first entered one of my groups I asked her why she sought help:

'I've lost interest in everything,' she said.

Jane had grown up in a lower-middle-class home in Detroit. Her father was a foreman at a General Motors plant. Her mother was a semi-invalid, and relied on Jane from an early age to help her with the housework. As Jane grew so did her mother's dependence on her.

When Jane was five years old her father began molesting her, and within a few years he was having regular intercourse with her. This went on until she was eighteen, when she married.

Jane's first child was stillborn, and she saw this as divine punishment for what she had done with her father, though she had never been a willing participant. She had been constantly depressed throughout her life, but the stillbirth pushed her over the edge – causing her to admit herself into a psychiatric hospital for several weeks. The admitting diagnosis: depressive neurosis with suicidal tendencies. Jane was close to her mother at the time, but was unable to confess the incest to her because she worried about her mother's health.

Eight years and two children later Jane finally told her mother about the incest. The middle-aged woman reacted noncommittally, saying merely, 'That's all past now. Put it behind you.' Though Jane's mother had separated from her husband she still loved him.

To Jane this nonchalance was cruelly unsympathetic. How could her mother be so casual about the ugliness of the incest?

Two years after Jane's confession her mother became terminally ill. On her deathbed she summoned Jane and made her promise to forgive her father. Jane had no alternative but to make the promise – one does not argue with a dying parent. Yet Jane blamed her father for the misery of her life, and could barely stand to see him, much less forgive him. The guilt over being unable to fulfill her promise brought her incest conflicts to the surface, and they were pulling her apart. This deathbed promise drove Jane back into the psychiatric hospital.

In group therapy we began to work out her feelings through role-playing (a method of therapy that I find particularly effective in treating incest patients). During the first session Jane played herself and another group member played her father. The result was a powerful display of hatred, rage, and an appeal for her right to dignity. In the following session she asked to do a scene with me playing her mother. Despite the fact that her mother had not known about the incest until Jane had confessed to it years later, Jane became livid, bitterly accusing her mother of neglect.

'Where were you when I needed you?' she cried. 'Why didn't you know what was going on? You were married to the man, how could you not know? Why didn't you protect me? I didn't have anyone to turn to – you seemed so cold, so far away. How could you do this to me?'

After this session, and others that were similar, Jane felt guilty about allowing herself to be angry at her 'sainted' dead mother. But clearly she placed a good deal of responsibility for the incest with her mother.

Jane eventually came to understand how her mother had neglected her family's emotional needs, how the woman had used her infirmity to push Jane into more than housekeeping duties, and how she had unfairly coerced Jane into making the deathbed promise as a means of ameliorating her own guilt.

As Jane worked out her feelings her improvement was dramatic. She entered the hospital disheveled, downcast, and uncaring, and left as a relatively confident woman. She began grooming and dressing carefully; she held her head high; and she stopped talking about the uselessness of living and of her own worthlessness.

Jane's mother's participation was entirely psychological. In some cases, however, the silent partner's physical actions may be so blatant that in retrospect it is difficult to believe she did not know what she was doing.

I. Kaufman and colleagues concluded from a 1954 eleven-case study that incestuous daughters 'felt free to return the father's affection sexually because the mother had unconsciously given them permission.' They cited as an example one mother who could not tolerate her husband's snoring and went to sleep in another room. 'Then out of concern that he would be lonely she put the daughter in her place in bed with the husband.' It is difficult to get any closer to outwardly condoning incestuous activities, yet it is still possible that this mother did not consciously want her daughter to have sex with her husband. Some mothers do.

THE ACTIVELY INVOLVED MOTHER

The actively involved mother spans a wide range of participation from subtle prodding to actual physical involvement. She does more than just set up the incest situation – at the very least she sets up the act itself. Her motives are usually identical to those of the silent partner, but it takes a more disturbed, perhaps psychotic personality to react to those motives consciously.

The actively participating mother tends to be a dependent woman. At first she leans on her husband, but as her daughter assumes more and more responsibility for household duties the mother shifts this dependence to her. The mother begins to resent her daughter, as if her daughter were stealing the maternal role instead of having it thrust upon her. As this resentment grows the mother becomes hostile toward her daughter, driving the girl closer to her father, and causing the mother to want to see her daughter punished, demeaned.

The mother's hostility, combined with her disturbed personality, can lead to varying degrees of consciously promoting incest. On the more innocent end of the scale is the mother who may try to persuade herself that there is nothing incestuous in what she is doing, but the facts argue to the contrary. I recently reviewed such a case with a police investigator who specializes in cases of sexually abused children.

Jackie Marcus

Fifteen-year-old Lynn Marcus had been apprehended by the police as a runaway. She told investigators that she had been a victim of incestuous rape by her father. Lynn's mother, Jackie, denied the possibility of incest, suggesting to the detectives that Lynn had made up the story because the girl wanted to live in a foster home 'for status.' Lynn apparently ran around with a 'tough' crowd.

Jackie admitted that Lynn had made similar allegations previously. Jackie had not believed her, and in fact had punished her for 'lying.' Yet when the police questioned Lynn's younger sister Sue they received similar allegations of sexual abuse. This seemed to startle Jackie. 'Sue never lies to me,' she said. Jackie was forced to accept the charges, but she still refused to cooperate in prosecuting her husband: 'I don't want to lose him. If there's some program to help him, okay. But I won't prosecute. If I have to choose between my husband and my children, I'll choose my husband – even if it means never seeing my children again.'

As evidence piled up from various interviews with family members a pattern of promoting incestuous sexuality began to emerge, much of it stemming from Jackie. For instance she persuaded the girls to shower with their father 'to conserve water.' On one occasion Lynn was talking about receiving a 'hickie' from a boy at school, and Jackie directed her husband to show Lynn 'what a real hickie is all about.' He sucked on Lynn's neck until a 'love-bite' appeared. On still another occasion Jackie told Lynn to remove her blouse and allow her father to feel her breasts 'for lumps.'

Clearly Jackie had consciously pushed Lynn into sexual activities with her father, which leads me to question the sincerity of Jackie's surprise when the police first confronted her with the allegation. Vehement denial is a normal reaction of mothers involved in incest, but Jackie was also quite capable of consciously lying for her husband, considering her remark about choosing him over her children if need be – a surprisingly frequent choice of these women. Sincere or not, Jackie was able to maintain that she was innocent because she did not directly participate in her daughter's rape.

ENCOURAGING RAPE

On the darker end of the scale is the mother whose hostility toward her daughter and lack of normal maternal instincts are so great that she actually participates in her daughter's sexual assault. I ran into a particularly dramatic example of this type of participation recently when I was asked to testify as an expert witness in the trial of a young woman who was accused (and eventually convicted) of first-degree murder in Bakersfield, California. She was said to have persuaded her fourteen-year-old son to shoot his father by telling the boy that the father had been sexually abusing the boy's thirteen-year-old sister.

The family situation at the time was tragic, but tragedy seemed to be the only end this young woman could have come to in view of the horrors of her childhood. I spent several hours interviewing her in jail, and she described how her own mother had, on several occasions, actually held her down while her stepfather had raped her.

When I think of the psychological barriers that must be broken down by such mothers it amazes me that as many as 6 percent of all incest cases involve their active participation (according to the Kinsey study).

In rare instances the mother is forced to participate by the aggressor. She is threatened either with violence or abandonment. In these cases the mother is invariably a dependent, infantile, passive woman who will tolerate any abuse to herself or her children to placate her husband. She often puts up with such abuse because it is the only kind of life she has ever known. Frequently she has been an incest victim herself, and has drifted into the familiar pattern of choosing an abusive mate. The combined guilt of her own incest and her daughter's can be shattering.

DISCOVERY AND DENIAL

The typical mother who discovers her husband and daughter are involved in incest finds herself in a position of having to take sides in a conflict between her husband and her daughter. This no-win position is complicated by the financial and emotional security her husband provides, as opposed to the trauma of betraying her child. She may become paralyzed by these alternatives, and sink into severe depression. She feels betrayed herself – an outsider in her own home. She feels inadequate, undesired, somehow guilty.

She frequently displaces her rage and frustration on her daughter. She becomes accusatory: 'You could have stopped it,' 'You must have wanted him to do it,' 'What do you want me to do – send him to jail and go on welfare?' At a time when her daughter most needs her support and understanding even the uninvolved mother may be so blinded by her own pain that she can only lash out.

The mother's reaction once the incest is revealed can be a key factor in determining the degree of damage her child will suffer. Unfortunately most mothers react with hostility, calling their daughters home-wreckers, liars, sluts.

No matter what the nature of the mother's involvement she still experiences guilt once incest is discovered. If she was uninvolved, she wonders what she had done wrong. If she was unconsciously involved, she senses her participation unconsciously, but consciously denies it. If she was consciously involved, and is not too psychotic to understand what she has done, she feels guilty about her activities. In all three cases this guilt triggers unconscious defenses.

The mother usually tries to deal with her guilt by projecting it onto her daughter, just as the silent partner passes along her maternal responsibilities. The mother is jealous of her daughter, who has become 'the other woman,' and she blames her daughter for breaking up the family. The bulk of her anger stems from her unconscious need to deny her own responsibility. Even if she admits her responsibility her denial stems from an unconscious need to rationalize her involvement and displace her guilt onto her daughter.

The mother's attempts at denial may be based on her need to keep the family together, on her financial or emotional dependence on her husband. She may make excuses for him – he was drunk, he was seduced, he just lost control. She will often try to handle the situation without calling in the authorities, giving her the power to blackmail her husband for his misdeeds. In this way she effects a transfer of power in the household, taking over the family reins. In essence she castrates her husband and further removes herself from the maternal role – the attempted escape which may have set up the incest in the first place.

Whether as a response to disbelief, guilt, or financial insecurity denial is the standard response of almost all victims' mothers when incest is first discovered. Jane's mother tried to effect a reconciliation between Jane and her father, as if nothing had transpired between them. Jackie refused to believe Lynn's accusation that her father had molested her, despite Jackie's own prodding of sexual activities between father and daughter. We will encounter the same types of denial throughout this book.

The tragedy of this denial is that the mother's participation in therapy is often crucial to the victim's treatment. The victim feels guilt over having betrayed her mother, and needs to be told by her mother that she is not responsible. Denial, however, prevents many mothers from going into therapy, for they see such participation as an admission of their own blame. The silent partner is notorious for refusing to participate in the rehabilitation process, which only increases her burden of guilt. For no matter how successful she is at denying her guilt she still carries it with her.

Only through treatment can a family deal with the explosiveness of the incest situation. Only through treatment will the mother escape her own corner of the incest hell – and, in the process, release her daughter.

6 · FATHER–DAUGHTER INCEST

Despite the progress of the women's rights movement over the last few years we still live in a man's world, and many men are still being raised to think of women as sex objects. Too often a father views his daughter as his sexual property, to exploit as he sees fit. In *Against Our Will* Susan Brownmiller describes this mentality: 'The taboo against father rape is superceded by a stronger, possibly older taboo – there shall be no outside interference in the absolute dictatorship of father rule.' This attitude was typified by a comment made to Los Angeles Sheriff's deputies several years ago by a man whom they had arrested for repeated sexual intercourse with his two teenage daughters. The man freely admitted his incestuous acts, remarking: 'It's getting pretty bad if a man can't raise his own fucking.'

This concept of daughters as sexual chattel is probably responsible for weakening the taboo against father–daughter incest compared to the taboos against other forms of incest. Father–daughter incest is by far the most common type of adult–child incest. When it occurs, because the father is the traditional source of family 'law,' the matter must often be dealt with outside the family – usually by the police.

Thus father–daughter cases are the ones which most often come to light and become the bases for the bulk of incest studies and statistics. Seventy-five percent of all reported incest cases involve fathers and daughters.

The actual rate of occurrence in the population is unclear, primarily because so many cases go unreported, even in confidential surveys. My colleagues have ventured guesses that range from 7.5 to 40 percent of all families with daughters.

In the preceding three chapters we have examined the members of the father–daughter incest triad – the victim, the aggressor, and the silent partner. In this chapter we will see them interact. This first case I will present, though factual, can serve as a classic case. All the motivations and reactions among the incest triad are not only clear from the story, but they are insightfully voiced by the victim herself. Rarely have I heard the dynamics of incest so explicitly laid out by a victim, especially one who has never been in treatment.

Freda Bennet

I met Freda Bennet at a party. She had heard about my book and volunteered her story.

Freda's hair is almost black, styled close to her head. Her eyes are hazel. She is a plain woman, but full of life, giving her an aura of beauty. She is a screenwriter who has written a few moderately successful films and occasionally has written for television. She lives in a comfortable old Spanish-style duplex with her aged cat and her twenty-two-year-old daughter, Kim. Her demeanor is cheerful.

Freda was born and raised in Hollywood, where her father was an actor. She recalls: 'My mother was a seamstress for a brassiere factory during the war. Afterwards she did piece work for them, bringing home forty or forty-five dollars a week, something like that. I have a sister, Jean, who is a year-and-a-half older than me. We were just us two girls and my mother much of the time – my dad would show up occasionally, always drunk.

'We lived in a bungalow court in the Hollywood hills. No bedroom – Murphy bed came down in the dining room. There was a living room – a sofa and chairs, a nine-by-twelve rug that just fit – and a kitchen and bathroom. That was it. When my dad showed up he slept on the couch. We girls slept on the Murphy bed with my mother in the middle.

'Jean was a good student. She did everything right. Got all the grades. "Why can't you be like Jean?" they'd always say. (My father never touched *her*.) Some people used to call her beanpole. She was tall, skinny, had freckles, brown eyes – I'm the only one in the family without brown eyes. We didn't look at all like sisters. I was always very heavy. I wore glasses. Kids always called me "fatty" or "four-eyes".

'My mother, on the other hand, looked like a beautiful Indian squaw, which is what she is. Her family is Indian, from Oklahoma. When she was younger she was often mistaken for Hedy Lamarr. She was five or ten years younger than my father, and she was *not* sharp. It's always been like she's in a shell; she doesn't see or hear half of what goes on.

'My father, on the other hand, was very sharp. He looked just like Rudolph Valentino. As a matter of fact he doubled for Valentino in a few films. He always had women hanging around him, and my mother was always upset over some shenanigans he was up to. All my mother could hope for was that he wouldn't bring them home with him, which he sometimes did.

'His sex life with my mother seemed active enough. I remember waking up in the middle of the night and wondering why I would hear him shouting, "dirty motherfucker," and thinking he was furious with her. But he was not at all; he just used abusive language when they had sex. At the time I didn't understand, but looking back it's clear what was going on.

'Their social life was nonexistent. They never went out; they never had friends in. I had a lot of friends, but I never brought people to my house. I never knew when my father would show up drunk or when my mother would look like she was about to have a nervous breakdown. I was really ashamed of how we lived.

'Though my life was pretty miserable in the house, I do have a lot of happy memories. I was always laughing and jolly, but I was also always in trouble. People were constantly complaining about me – landladies, neighbors. I was always doing something I wasn't supposed to – smoking in the garage, throwing orange peels on the pavement, things like that.

'Despite all my mischief I only remember one spanking as a child. I guess there were many slaps that I forgot; I *was* disciplined. But I remember one time – I was five or six – when I crossed the street on my roller skates. I had been told not to, but I felt that was an unreasonable restriction to place on a six-year-old woman of the world. When my dad found out he beat me with a wooden hanger. I couldn't sit down for six weeks. I had horrible welts, warped skin in some places. I lost control of my bladder and urinated all over everything. I don't know why, but I think now there was a sexual motivation on his part. It was just too intense a thing, too brutal. I have no positive memories at all about my father, just negative ones.

'He was a mean person. He would hit my mother all the time. I think it was only because of her that he hardly ever hit us. It wasn't so much that she was against our being hit as it was that she felt if he wanted control over our discipline he had to contribute to our livelihood. She had a good wedge there. She kept the family going. He'd squander all the money he could get his hands on with his drinking and gambling. Then he'd go out and hang some paper – he got my mother to pass some bad checks too.

'They were always fighting. I remember he stabbed her once. They were having an argument. The bed was down in the dining room and my father was sitting on it. My mother squeezed by him, around the bed, and she felt something in her back and she thought that he had hit her. Later she found blood there and she didn't want to go to a doctor or the police or anything like that, so she went to a pharmacist, who was a family friend. He patched her up. It wasn't very deep and my father hadn't slashed her or anything, he had just poked her with a knife, stuck her. But he would beat her all the time.

'The first time I remember anything funny going on with my father – and I really think this is the first time I remember, not the first time anything happened – I was about seven. I was asleep in the Murphy bed with my mother and my sister and I woke up and started pulling away – I realized I was being touched and started pulling away. And then I realized it was my father touching my vagina and I continued to pull away. He told me that I should not kid myself because when I was asleep I was enjoying it. He said that I had been making sounds in my sleep that indicated how much I was enjoying his touching me, moaning and so forth. He spoke in a whisper, so he wouldn't wake the others. I didn't know what was going on, so I tried to relax and allowed him to continue.

'After that first time there would be frequent contact whenever anybody wasn't looking. If I was alone with him, or even with the whole family around, he would touch me or he would reach over to kiss me good-bye and French-kiss me instead. He was constantly pulling me sexually. He would not let me escape the sexual aspect of him. I would try to please him in little ways because I didn't know or understand, it was confusing to me. But there were moments I remember enjoying. I mean, I was the ugly one, and this was the closest thing I had ever experienced to love because I really did feel unloved. The only physical affection that I remember were the incidents with my father, which I came to think of as competition with my mother after a while. I realized that these were the same kinds of caresses that she would get when he was in a good mood, or if he was pleased with her. And then I started to get them. It was the only thing I was getting that my sister didn't have, and that was important to me too.

'I only remember touching him once, and I was appalled at what happened. The thing erupted, at which point he told me not to be afraid, that that was normal. But there was never any intercourse. I remember when I was eight he tried and it just wouldn't work. I was just too small. It hurt. He was very upset and I was afraid he was going to hit me, but he didn't.

'My mother should have known what was going on, she had all the signs she needed. But my mother is the type of person who sees what she wants to see and hears what she wants to hear and crawls through life trying not to have a landslide cave in on her. He wasn't to be trusted, but she trusted him. She trusted him too much as far as I'm concerned. One of my feelings of rage toward her was that I felt that I should have been protected more by her. I would have killed anyone who ever approached my daughter when she was little. Even if I only had a suspicion, it would be my fault if I didn't keep that person away from her. I feel cheated that I didn't have that protection as a child. I feel that the incest has taken its toll in pain and guilt and emotional chaos. It shouldn't have happened. But my mother is a very weak person. She can barely take care of herself, let alone anybody else. She had no business having children.

'When I was about eight I remember my mother asking me about this little girl, about my age, who lived with her family in the garage in back of our house. She was working around to something – she didn't come right out and ask me anything. It was like we were sitting down and having a little conversation. She said, "Does Daddy ever play with Caroline, or does he ever go back there when she's alone, or does he ever touch her?" When I finally got the idea of what she was trying to find out I said, "No, he doesn't do that to her, but to me."

'You have to understand that I never talked to my mother. She just didn't talk to anyone. So I was excited just having a conversation with her. All I wanted was to tell her what she wanted to know, and once I understood what she was asking I was delighted to be able to tell her. I didn't even think that I had brought up something dirty. It just came out. And since I was so innocent about it, so honest, she really couldn't ignore it anymore. She didn't say much, but I was made to feel ashamed.

I could just feel it – something's wrong, something's bad, something's dirty. The first thing she did was blame me.

'I didn't consciously realize what I had done until my teens, and even then I didn't understand it. I had come to enjoy that sexual attention because I never knew any other kind, and I looked to people for that for the rest of my life. I remember my father telling my mother that I would be pregnant by the time I was twelve. He didn't miss by much. I got pregnant when I was fourteen-and-a-half. That was another horror story altogether, involving a quack abortionist. I almost died of peritonitis.

'Anyway, my mother finally divorced him. It wasn't just the incest – she even told me that she felt that was a father's duty. Her father did the same things to my aunts. But sometimes she would say things on the one hand and do something else on the other. Obviously she couldn't handle the whole thing. It was a culmination of everything.

'The divorce was probably the best thing that ever happened to my mother. Yet I was convinced for years after that she was still in love with him.

'So I went through school seeking the only affection that I had ever learned. During my teen years, and twenties, and thirties there was a wealth of men. I was very promiscuous, and very attractive, too. Hundreds of men went to bed with me, hundreds of them. I can remember some-one new would ask me for a date and I promised myself that I wouldn't go to bed on the first night. But I always did. I wanted to. I totally enjoyed myself. I always have. It was impossible to conceal my enjoyment. I was a bad girl; at that time you just didn't do that. And it took its toll in friends. I can remember I got kicked out of a club, some girls' club with a Latin name. Things like that were always happening.

'They eventually kicked me out of high school because I got pregnant. They didn't like pregnant people walking around the quad at Hollywood High. I decided to have the baby this time, and Kim was born when I was seventeen.

'My father finally went to Alcoholics Anonymous and got himself straightened out, at least as far as his drinking was concerned. I remember calling him when I was about to marry, wanting to set everything straight, hopefully to construct a family out of all this chaos, and to invite him to the wedding. He said he wanted to see me. I was twenty-two at the time. He said I should come over to his place, he had a pool and we could change in his apartment – the tone of his voice was very explicit, sexual. I thought, here I was getting married, a minister and everything, even though Kim was five years old at the time – it was something very important to me – and I got this response from him.

'That is when I put him out of my life. I never spoke to him again. I just wouldn't leave myself open for it. It was too traumatic for me. It's been five years now since he died, and it's only lately that I've allowed myself to even think about him. Now my phone is listed for the first time in my life because I don't have to worry that he'll call.

'He would always call and make allusions to sex, trying to persuade me that incest was perfectly natural. He would try to prove it by saying it was in the Bible. He wouldn't quote any specific passages – he was not a Bible-quoting man – he would just assure me that it was in there somewhere.

'The whole thing affected my life profoundly. It still colors everything. I've never been in analysis or anything like that. I don't know if I'm completely whole now. I don't know that I've completely worked out the guilt, even now. But as you gain knowledge these things work themselves out, I guess. It's just the growing process and being exposed to the world.

'I feel that I understand, I mean rationally, but emotionally the things come back in strange ways. For instance, I absolutely trusted my husband. I never for a moment worried about him taking any liberties with Kim. But he was never alone with her anyway. Never. If there was ever a choice about whether she would stay home with him or go shopping with me, she came with me. And of course I never let her spend time with my father. I don't even think they ever met. If we were at a social gathering at my sister's or something and he would show up I'd just whisk Kim up and split. I didn't even want her to see him. I'm glad that he's dead.'

Freda lives a fairly solitary life today. Her marriage lasted only five months. In retrospect she feels her husband was a father figure – he was an older man whose last name was the same as her father's first name. She doesn't think she will remarry, saying that she is satisfied living as a single woman and that she mistrusts men.

I am in no position to judge the quality of Freda's life, but she admits she needs marijuana and alcohol to cope with the pressures she feels.

Her story brings into sharp focus the conflicting feelings of the classic incest victim. She enjoyed her father's caresses as the only affection she'd every really known, yet she felt guilty about the incest. She felt competitive with her mother and unable to communicate with her. She became promiscuous, yet mistrusted men. She was enraged at her father's betrayal of her trust and violation of her physical integrity, and at her mother's failure to protect her.

Freda's father, too, was classic in his aggressor role. He was obviously an unhappy man. Perhaps he was frustrated over doubling for Valentino instead of *being* Valentino. He was certainly compulsive in his pursuit of gratification – gambling, drinking, chasing women. But he seemed to find no fulfillment. He wanted to be *somebody*, but outside his home he was just another would-be actor. So he fed his fragile ego by becoming a tyrant, beating his wife and children, living his life with no regard for anyone else.

It is unlikely that he turned to Freda merely because he wanted another sexual object. He apparently had a steady stream of sexual affairs to keep him busy, and between them he seemed to have an active sex life with his wife. But neither his affairs nor his wife met his needs for tenderness and love. He expected these to be the profits of family life, so it was to his family that he instinctively turned. Of course this was not something that he did consciously. He did not understand what his needs were, and he did not know how to satisfy them.

Unconsciously he was drawn to his family, but he could not communicate with his wife – any attempt at conversation inevitably evolved into argument. With his older daughter – the model of propriety, the 'good girl' – he could feel no spiritual kinship. But Freda was the wild one, the roly-poly cute one, the impulsive one. He might have seen signs of his own character in her. Freda was the one who might understand him, who might sympathize with him. She was the one to whom he might be able to relate. But he was not a talker. His social conversations were demonstrations of bravado; his family conversations were demonstrations of power. He was a man in the Latin-lover mold. The only thing he knew to seek from women was sex. So that is what he sought from Freda. With her there were none of the obscenities, the roughness, the passion that there had been with his wife. He vainly sought tenderness from someone who, like himself, had no idea of what it was.

He died still trying to seduce his daughter. In a way he was seeking a substitute for his wife. Freda felt this, and she came to regard her relationship with her father as 'competition with my mother.' Her mother, the silent partner, must have also felt this competition, and later blamed Freda for her divorce. Of course her charges were not only unjustified, they were her tools of denial, to cover up her own guilt. She sensed that her husband's desperate yearnings reflected her own failure to satisfy his needs. She sensed her own role in the family breakdown.

Freda, too, understood the silent partner role; this was the source of her rage toward her mother. Her mother could have protected Freda from her father. Instead she withdrew, not talking to anyone, expressing no love or affection. She, too, had no real understanding of what a loving household should be.

In an incestuous situation the nature of the emotional relationship among father, daughter, and mother is crucial. Sex is merely the casing of the incest bomb – family emotions provide the explosives. Because the incest trauma is so intrinsically tied to family emotions a one-time occurrence of incest can be as destructive as a long-term relationship. Betrayal need not be repeated to be destructive. Lynnelle Matson's story is a case in point.

Lynnelle Matson

Lynnelle entered one of my therapy groups a few years ago as a result of a drinking problem. She had admitted herself into the hospital for treatment. She is a petite, attractive, fifty-year-old woman with short-cropped blond hair and hazel, almost metallic eyes. Her voice is deep and resonant, yet girlish.

Lynnelle was born in a small town in New Hampshire, out of wedlock, to a sixteen-year-old working mother. She never met her father. For the first ten years of her life she was shuffled back and forth among her grandmother and various aunts and uncles. She felt uncomfortable around her family, unwanted.

'I remember when I first went to live with my Uncle Stan,' she recalls. 'I had only been there for a day or two and they were talking about putting up a stand to sell jelly. I thought they were talking about selling "Nellie," which was my nickname then, so I hid in the attic. I was terrified. I always felt inferior to the other kids in the family because at Christmas I would always get hand-me-down clothes and toys.'

When Lynnelle was ten she finally went to live with her mother – a beautiful, dark-complexioned woman. Less than a month later her mother married a salesman named Jason Warren.

'He was the only one of her boyfriends I didn't like,' Lynnelle says. 'I felt kind of sick about that marriage, I really did. I couldn't put my finger on why, but just didn't feel comfortable around him.'

A few months later the family packed up and moved to California. At this time Lynnelle began to study the piano seriously. As a young child she had been considered something of a prodigy for her ability to pick up fairly complicated piano pieces by ear. Now her talent was being developed by a competent teacher, and she was playing extraordinarily well.

'About a year after we moved to California my first stepbrother was born. That changed the household quite a bit. I felt even more out of place. At first they had been honeymooners, and they wanted to be by themselves. But after my brother was born my mother and father seemed to resent my being around. Like if I came in and they were playing with the baby, and I tried to join them or something, my mother would say, "Can't you go and do something, pick up your room or play outside?" I just felt like they were trying to ignore me. I always had that feeling.'

When she was thirteen her piano teacher arranged a solo recital at a large auditorium in Los Angeles. For the first time Lynnelle's mother seemed to be excited about something Lynnelle was doing. They went shopping together for a new dress and shoes, and a caterer was hired for a party after the recital. Finally the big day arrived.

'I was nervous. I was terribly nervous. And my mother, who had been freaking out about this recital, getting the dress and everything, didn't come. That made me feel awful. She got a mysterious "flu attack." I think she was smashed. She was an alcoholic. When she didn't show up I had such a lump in my throat. At least my father was there.

'There must have been five hundred people there. When I first walked on stage it was like taking a deep breath. I was so little, and it was such a big stage with such a big piano on it and all those people. I had never played a Steinway Concert Grand before and it was absolutely huge.

When I first sat down, all I could think of was "Oh, my God, I have so many things to play." It was such a relief to get through it.

'My stepfather was very proud – I think everybody from his company was there. Afterwards he came up and he was really feeling no pain, he had had some drinks, and he told me how proud he was of me. That was the first time he had ever complimented me, and it felt really good.

'After the recital we went home and my mother had a woman serving things because a lot of people came back for the celebration. I was surprised because it was all for me, and a lot of them brought me gifts – like it was a birthday party. It was my shining hour, that's for sure. But my mother was asleep. It hurt that she wasn't there, but everything else was so perfect. I had never been so happy before! But even at the height of the festivities I kept thinking someone was going to send me out any minute. I wasn't used to all the attention. It was so strange, so wonderful, like a dream.

'Finally everyone went home. My mother and my little brother were asleep. I felt like a princess in my new dress, and my father came up and gave me a ginger ale. We sat down and he said, "I'm really proud of you. You looked so pretty and you played so well. And I know how hard you worked." Then he put his arms around me and it felt great. He had never shown me any affection before.

'But then he started getting huffy and puffy, and he started feeling around under my dress. I can recall thinking, "God, I hate to screw this up, this warmth." But I knew things were getting out of hand. I don't remember if he said anything, I blocked it out of my mind. I just remember thinking his breath didn't smell good. I didn't want it to go on but I didn't want to screw up the good feelings he had for me. Then he penetrated me. It was so painful. I was scared. I felt sick, physically sick in my beautiful big balloon. I had had such good feelings and then ... I get weepy just thinking about it now. It was so horrible – one moment the incredible bliss and love that I had always wanted, then in an instant all the pain and fear and nausea. It was both the best and the worst day of my life.

'Afterwards he said, "Oh, I'm sorry. I'm sorry and we're going to forget this ever happened." I didn't want to forget it, but there was nothing I could do. I couldn't tell my mother and get that drunken rage blown at me. I just kept thinking, "why did this happen?"

'Even today I have trouble trusting a man. I find it particularly hard now for me to think a man is on the level with me.'

Lynnelle's stepfather never again molested her, yet that one brief occurrence stained her relations with men for the rest of her life, distorting her feelings to the point where her relationships repeatedly failed. The incest was the final trauma for an already needy and frightened child. The fact that it occurred on the most important day of her life virtually guaranteed that she would come to believe nothing good could last for her. She made that a self-fulfilling prophecy. Her relationships with men tend to seesaw. She pursues a man until he begins to respond. Then she backs down and rejects his advances. When he retreats she resumes her pursuit. Her feelings never seem to level off, the seesaw never stops.

This problem alone does not reflect the depth of her pain. The nagging guilt and self-doubt plague her continuously – these drove her to drink about five years ago. 'My coping mechanism just went out of whack,' she says. After three years she grew disgusted with her dependence on alcohol, and checked herself into the hospital for treatment. There, for the first time, her incest experience came out during a group therapy session.

'I can't say that it really felt good to finally admit the incest,' she says. Her eyes redden at the thought. 'No, I can't say that it felt good at all. Certainly a lot of the problems that I feel – lack of confidence in myself, no motivation to get out and do, no trust in people – are due to all the crap I had in growing up. I had to play like things were okay, but they really weren't. I was so used to playing the game that when the incest came out in group I got sick to my stomach and had to run out. As a matter of fact, I'm not really feeling too good right now. It's that hard to think about it, even after thirty-seven years.'

Nevertheless she has recently begun a secure, comfortable job with a large corporation, and she has begun dating again – though cautiously. Lynnelle's admission, no matter how painful it was to make, was her first step toward a better life. She still has a distance to go, but she is traveling in the right direction.

Her case is typical of one-time occurrences. Once the trust inherent in a parent–child relationship is destroyed, it is very difficult to resurrect. Though most incestuous relationships continue after the incest taboo has been breached, one-time occurrences clearly can be just as traumatic.

You may have noticed that Lynnelle referred to Jason Warren sometimes as her stepfather and sometimes as her father in the interview. The discrepancy illustrates how the distinction between father and stepfather blurs in the eyes of a child. For all practical purposes he was her father. She had lived with him as patriarch almost as long as she had lived with her mother. He provided for Lynnelle and her mother, his word was the law of the household, and though she claimed to have always disliked him she responded eagerly when he showed affection for her. She called him 'daddy,' understanding nothing about bloodlines. On the happiest night of her life, when her mother was typically absent, both physically and emotionally, she turned to him as her father for love, affection, and recognition.

The incest trauma was as real to Lynnelle as it would have been if the aggressor had been her blood-father. And it hurt deeply. In a remark that echoes something Freda said Lynnelle reveals how deeply: 'If any man ever touches my daughter I'll probably kill him.' When asked how old her daughter must be before she revokes this threat Lynnelle says – perhaps only half-jokingly – 'thirty-six'.

Lynnelle had one more outstanding symptom. She suffered debilitating migraine headaches repeatedly since high school. I find this symptom in nearly half of my cases. I consider it an expression of self-punishment. Headaches have long been recognized by psychotherapists as symptoms of repressed rage. My therapeutic experience indicates that headaches can also result from sexual tension caused by incest conflicts. When those conflicts are treated the headaches are among the first symptoms to disappear. Lynnelle's headaches went away rather dramatically after she confronted her incest in group therapy.

Both cases we have examined so far in this chapter involved victims whose incestuous experiences remained hidden for several decades. Often, however, as in the following case, the victim's reaction is so powerful that she requires immediate treatment following an incest trauma, and the incest is consequently revealed. This happened to fifteen-year-old Carrie McPherson, an angelic-looking girl who became grossly psychotic after her mother discovered she had had intercourse with her father. Ideally, in such cases the therapist should treat the entire family, but few cases work out that way, as Carrie's story illustrates.

Carrie McPherson

I first met Carrie in one of my adolescent groups. Her personality was fragmented, she was hearing voices, and her thoughts were totally disorganized – a textbook case of paranoid schizophrenia. But the textbooks never prepare you for the emotional impact of a damaged child. She was needy, clinging, frightened, haunted, and projecting a sadness that touched everyone she spoke to.

She wept as she told the group about having sex with her father shortly after she had gone to live with him – she couldn't get along with her cold, rejecting mother. It was unclear whether the incest had occurred on several occasions or only a few – her story came out in disjointed bits and pieces. But one phrase kept popping up throughout her narrative: 'Mother, it wasn't my fault!' If only Carrie had really believed that.

Carrie's mother is a key figure in this drama. In Carrie's admissions record the examining social worker described Carrie as 'a youngster who has not had a secure home, who appears not to be overly intelligent, who has not functioned well in her peer group, and who became severely disturbed after her mother discovered her incestuous relationship with the father. Carrie feels very torn between her parents and very ambivalent in the relationship with her father. It appeared essential to get mother involved to share her anger and then be able to accept Carrie. However, mother was too threatened by any kind of treatment plan to cooperate.'

The police report provides additional evidence of Mrs McPherson's refusal to become involved: 'Mrs McPherson declined to discuss the matter, stating that it was over and done with, and in the past.' This type of reluctance is common – and tragic. Not only will Carrie's father not be prosecuted – Carrie is too sick to testify, and her mother refuses to press charges – but Carrie's treatment will be severely hampered by her mother's refusal to participate.

Carrie's father simply left the state, and has not been heard from since. His absence, too, is unfortunate for Carrie, for she needs him to relieve her of responsibility.

Even though her parents had divorced, Carrie's repeated denial to her mother – 'It wasn't my fault' – shows that she felt she was usurping her mother's role. This is a great source of guilt for Carrie, despite her denials. That is why her mother's forgiveness is so important to her, and why her therapy is so difficult without her mother's participation. Carrie needs her mother's love and support, but as a result of her mother's refusal to participate in treatment, Carrie's hospitalization may be extended for years. Perhaps she will be strong enough to deal with her guilt and recognize her innocence one day, but she will have to reach this point the hard way – alone.

The victim of father–daughter incest is frequently alone with her problem. The family situation usually does not permit her to seek help, so she bottles her trauma. Incest is rarely the victim's only trauma, but it is the problem most difficult to share, so it tends to fester in secrecy and shame. This process sometimes continues even after the incest is discovered, as in Carrie's case.

In presenting the cases in this book I have a dual purpose: to educate the public about the nature of incest, and to show incest participants that they are *not* alone, that their symptoms are normal and treatable.

7 · MOTHER–SON INCEST

Mother–son incest, when it is represented in the arts or in the erotic media, is generally treated lightly, like a simple love affair that just happens to be between mother and son. A prime example of this is French filmmaker Louis Malle's beautiful *Murmur of the Heart*, a passionate story about a mid-teenage boy who ends up making love with his mother. When Malle wrote and directed the film in 1971, it aroused quite a controversy – the incestuous affair was depicted in a tender, benign light.

This theme found dubious validation in the Christmas, 1977, issue of *Penthouse* magazine, in which journalist Philip Nobile wrote an article about incest and alleged that in most cases mother–son incest is actually *beneficial* to the participants. A good deal of Nobile's evidence came from a researcher whose only credentials – which Nobile wishfully called 'impressive' – are that he has a Ph.D. in political science, he is a former board member of the National Organization for Women, and he has authored a book on new male roles. With absolutely no background in psychology or sociology this researcher found that mother–son incest 'represents 10 percent of the incidence [of all incest] and is 70 percent positive.'

In reality the dynamics of mother–son incest are probably the most involved, the least understood, and the most subtly traumatic of all forms of incest. I think it is absurd to suggest that the sexual attraction between mother and son – upon which Freud based his Oedipal theory, and which he saw as the core of human neurosis – could be acted out without severe psychological repercussions. Such acting out is like playing Russian roulette with five barrels loaded.

The belief that mother–son incest can be harmless stems from the fact that such incest is almost always tender and loving. Where an incestuous father can force himself on his daughter, an incestuous mother must seduce (or allow herself to be seduced by) her son, for if he is not sensually aroused he cannot maintain an erection. This mandatory tenderness makes it difficult to comprehend the emotional pain and unconscious conflicts that both lead to and result from the incest.

THE FATHER

The family triad I have discussed in father–daughter incest does not apply in mother–son cases. Instead of a silent partner there is usually an absent partner. In probably 95 percent of all mother–son cases the father is either no longer part of the nuclear family or is frequently away from home. This makes mother–son incest much more of a direct relationship between aggressor and victim than father–daughter incest is. There is no third party.

THE MOTHER

The physical absence of the father from a home where his presence, for various psychological reasons, is needed, often drives the mother to seek a substitute. She is generally a highly dependent woman; she needs a man. For moral reasons, as in father–daughter cases, she may not consider looking outside the family for sexual or emotional gratification – adultery is *twice* forbidden in the Ten Commandments, while incest is not even mentioned. Instead she slowly maneuvers her son into his father's role.

She may feel painfully rejected by her husband's absence, and try to negate that rejection by reliving their romance as it was when it first blossomed – this time with her son. Her son may resemble her husband as she remembers him in his youth, making the role transition that much easier for her to accept. Her need is as much emotional as sexual, and there is already a strong bond of love between her son and herself. That bond need be only slightly reshaped for her son to fill in for her absent husband.

Though she knows, at least unconsciously, that the incestuous relationship is wrong, her emotions overpower her. She suffers enormous guilt, which she denies by insisting that the relationship is one of special love. She swears her son to secrecy because no one else could possibly understand the depth of their love, she explains. She becomes extremely possessive and overprotective.

THE SON

The son, who might otherwise rebel against such possessiveness, now revels in it, for his sexual awakening (these victims are usually virgins, around puberty) has aroused in him passions that he has never before experienced, passions that he now associates with mother. His mother is the answer to all his fantasies, the fulfillment of his Oedipal desires.

As we discussed in Chapter Two, Freud theorized that the child longs to sleep with his mother and take his father's place. The mother–son incest victim has done just that. By stepping into his father's shoes the son symbolically becomes at the same time both his father and his father's rival. He is torn between guilt, desire, love, and hate. He loves his mother yet he hates her for the guilt she has created in him by allowing the role transformation to take place. Because there is no element of force involved the boy almost invariably comes away with crushing guilt feelings, for he must accept his share of the blame without the mitigating excuse of having been violated.

Such guilt may become an obstacle in any relationships he tries to initiate with women for the rest of his life, for every woman will remind him of his mother. In addition his mother's possessiveness isolates him from his peers, often rendering him insecure and extremely self-conscious. He never learns how to develop a normal relationship with a woman, how to communicate, how to flirt, and so he feels uncomfortable around women. This discomfort often turns to resentment. The victim may become a mysogynist, a wife beater, a daughter abuser, a rapist, or a murderer. Or he may react by forming homosexual relationships.

If his resentment turns inward, as it usually does with father–daughter victims, the son becomes self-destructive. He assumes he is not good enough for the women he meets, and he doubts his own ability to maintain an erection. He has learned to find sexual security and pleasure only in his mother's arms. As a result many victims become impotent.

THREE PATTERNS OF MOTHER–SON INCEST

The symptoms I have been describing do not necessarily derive from intercourse between mother and son. There are three forms that mother–son incest can take, two of which involve no intercourse at all. In fact the first pattern of incest would hardly be called incest by most people, yet the symptoms are just as traumatic for the victim as is actual incestuous intercourse.

In its most innocent form mother–son incest may entail no sexual contact at all. Mother and son may sleep in the same bed, dress and undress together, perhaps even bathe together, but that's as far as it goes. The mother sees nothing wrong in this relationship, but the son may begin to have erotic dreams about his mother from the incidental physical contact they have. These may be wet dreams. When he is awake he may fantasize about possessing her sexually. This leads to an excessive attachment to his mother, which can isolate him socially as surely as if they were having regular intercourse.

The key to the trauma is the son's role change. If the son sleeps in his father's spot in bed, becomes his mother's social escort, and is the subject of subtle sexual flirtation, he not only moves into his father's role, but that role is confounded by sexual frustration. The fact that sexual intercourse is taboo in this relationship often conditions him to reject intercourse in any relationship, making him impotent and fearful of women.

The second form of mother–son incest still falls short of intercourse, but sexual contact is more overt. Contact often begins relatively innocently, with the mother perhaps stimulating an infantile erection in her son out of curiosity. But as time moves on this stimulation becomes regular, and takes on sexual implications for her. She continues to bathe him long after he is able to bathe himself, and he allows her to because he enjoys the sexual stimulation, and he relishes the seductiveness of his mother as a result of his Oedipal yearnings. When he reaches puberty she begins to manipulate him to ejaculation. This is generally the extent of sexual contact. Again the son is sexually frustrated at the limits of this relationship, yet those limits become habitual, making him impotent with other women. His frustration makes him bitter and resentful of women.

The third form of mother–son incest is very rare. I have treated only two such cases in my entire practice. I refer to regular intercourse between mother and son. Though it is the most overt form of mother–son incest its effects on the victim are not necessarily more traumatic than the effects of the other two forms. The following case is typical in many aspects.

Jackson Carter

Jackson Carter is a plain, baldish, honest-looking man of thirty-eight. Married, with three children – two girls and a boy – he's a successful businessman, holding the number two position in a manufacturing firm that employs more than a thousand people. He lives in Atlanta, Georgia, where he was born.

When Jackson turned thirty he began to suffer from intense headaches. These were totally incapacitating headaches, rendering Jackson unable to think through the pain. Doctors examined him for allergies, brain tumors, hypertension, and neurological disorders, but could find no physiological cause.

His headaches began to take on predictable patterns. His secretary at work was an older woman, extremely efficient and experienced, and a bit motherly in her manner. Whenever she would make a minor mistake he would blow it out of proportion, going into an uncontrollable rage, then wind up with a headache. This same pattern of rage and headaches occurred with his wife.

His headaches began to develop whenever he became angry with his son, and occasionally with his daughters. They would also strike when his mother would call or drop by.

At about the same time he began to have trouble maintaining an erection during intercourse with his wife, so he restricted their sexual activities to petting and oral sex. His wife reluctantly agreed to these new sexual rules, sensing a problem but not really understanding what it was.

In an effort to alleviate his sexual frustrations he began to frequent pornographic movie houses. He would drape his overcoat across his lap and masturbate in the theater. This, too, created tension, for he knew that because of his professional and social position, if he were caught, he would be ruined. He imagined front-page newspaper stories denouncing him as a pervert. But he found a certain satisfaction in seeing his sexual fantasies on film – sadistic fantasies toward women, fantasies of manipulation and power, of domination. He hated himself for his pornographic/masturbatory habits, yet he could not give them up.

His tensions and guilt finally forced him to seek psychiatric help. When he was 33 he entered therapy with a colleague of mine. From the start Jackson was a difficult patient. He refused either to lie down or to relax, but instead sat bolt upright, completely tense. He discussed his childhood only reluctantly, and for several months mentioned nothing about his mother, and certainly nothing about incest. He spoke about dreams of violence, of being chased, of combat, and he would often see himself in these dreams as being a boy again. He would talk about his work, about his fights with his secretary, about his headaches. But his talk was all superficial. He refused to delve into anything painful. Often he would develop headaches during therapy, usually when he was prodded to talk about his mother, his secretary, or his wife.

After six months he finally admitted frequenting pornographic theaters. By digging into Jackson's pornographic fantasies the therapist for the first time learned that Jackson's relationship with his wife precluded intercourse. But when these sexual questions were pursued Jackson would invariably develop a headache and be unable to continue. The therapist kept pointing out that the headaches were Jackson's way of punishing himself and preventing himself from confronting the thoughts that he needed to sort out.

Together they kept digging into Jackson's psyche until one day Jackson let slip the fact that his mother had asked him to sleep in her bed because she was afraid of the dark. But then he changed the subject.

When the therapist asked Jackson to tell him more about sleeping with his mother Jackson was hit by a tremendous headache and was unable to continue the session. Over the next few sessions his story slowly came out.

Jackson's father was a clerk in a stockbroker's office, and his mother worked part-time as a waitress. Together they maintained a comfortable, stable lower-middle-class home in a small apartment building. Jackson was their only child, and his childhood was rather ordinary. His parents got along fairly well, he did well enough to get by in school, he had many friends, and he seemed happy and well-adjusted.

His mother was a small, pretty, quiet woman who never seemed to rest. As was traditional at that time, she lived uncomplainingly for her family, seeing her role as that of a server, a nurturer. Her husband was her rock, her island of strength in the midst of a baffling cosmopolitan world. She gave him all the support, love, tenderness, sex, and good food she could muster. When she wasn't busy pampering him she would pamper Jackson.

The Carters went on family outings occasionally, and Mr and Mrs

Carter went out dancing or to a movie at least once a week. For all practical purposes they were an unremarkable family.

When the Korean War broke out Jackson's father enlisted in the army and was sent overseas. Jackson's mother went to work full-time to support them. When Jackson was eleven his father wrote home to announce that he had fallen in love with another woman and wanted a divorce. His wife was shocked, and understandably depressed, but she granted the divorce without a struggle.

A pall settled over the Carter household. Mrs Carter continued to work and maintain her home for Jackson's sake, but her zeal disappeared. Jackson sensed this new sadness and, loving his mother as he did, tried to console her. He assured her in his childish way that he would take care of her. 'We don't need him,' he would say. He became more affectionate as he learned that this would make her smile, and she seemed to depend on his affection.

Jackson felt her becoming dependent on him, if only in small ways. After they went out for dinner or to a movie she would ask him to turn on the lights before she would enter the apartment. She would complain of her fear of the dark, or of strange noises, or of insects, and Jackson would reassure her as if he were the adult and she the child.

About six months after the divorce a violent thunderstorm so frightened Mrs Carter that she asked Jackson – then twelve – to sleep with her in her bed. She found this so comforting that he moved in permanently – allegedly as a guard against the dark and the night sounds and stray bugs.

'Sometime after the first few weeks of sleeping with her,' Jackson recalls, 'I woke up with an erection, so I went into the bathroom and masturbated. This happened a few times a week for several months until one night I woke up and my mother had her hand on my penis and was fondling it. We had intercourse that same night.

'After that we slept together almost every night. I felt incredible; I was on top of the world. Here I was a twelve-year-old kid having this wonderful sexual affair with a beautiful woman, escorting her about town – I was playing dad. I was the man of the house. While other kids were still trying on their fathers' clothes I had actually stepped into his shoes. I loved it. I was in heaven.

'Then all of a sudden my world crumbled. The war ended, all these servicemen were coming home, and my mother began dating other men.

After our relationship had been going on for about two years she all of a sudden married some jerk veteran, and that was that. I never again slept in her bed, and our physical relationship became so awkward that I was afraid to even hug her. I was crushed, but I didn't say a word. Not a word. I may have been only fourteen, but I still saw myself as "a man," so I bottled it all up inside.'

Jackson dropped out of school when he was sixteen and, against his mother's wishes, enlisted in the army. By the time he left the army four years later he had lost almost all contact with his mother. She and his stepfather had moved to Oregon to try their hand at farming, and Jackson rarely corresponded with them. A postcard at Christmas was their only tie.

At twenty-three he married an attractive, intelligent woman who bore two daughters in the first two years of their marriage. Their third child, a son, was born when Jackson was twenty-eight. He had just bought a new house in the suburbs, and had enough business and family responsibilities to keep his hands full, so he was unhappy about this third child. It had been an 'accident.' He felt pangs of hostility when his wife would pamper the new baby.

Going from job to job Jackson slowly climbed the corporate ladder. He repeatedly worked his way up to the number-two spot wherever he worked, but never quite mustered the effort to make the final step. Instead he would move to another, larger company.

When Jackson turned thirty his mother and stepfather moved back to Atlanta. It was during this period that he first began to suffer from the headaches and other symptoms that eventually led him into therapy.

Over the several months that it took Jackson to reveal his story and understand how it had been cropping up symbolically in his life his headaches began to recede, until finally they disappeared altogether. His other symptoms took a bit longer, but they, too, responded to treatment.

As he sorted through his past in therapy he gradually came to understand many of his problems. He learned that his rage at his secretary or his wife was actually suppressed rage toward his mother for subjecting him to so much guilt and then rejecting him. When his son was born he feared a replay, between his son and his wife, of his own experience and his jealousy led to hostility. With his mother's return to Atlanta, intercourse with his wife became too closely linked to memories of his incestuous relationship, so he had problems with sexual performance. The sadistic fantasies that the pornographic movies allowed him to indulge in were expressions of more rage toward his mother. And the headaches were merely his way of repressing taboo thoughts whenever his interaction with his wife or secretary brought back memories of his anger and frustration toward his mother.

In his career, too, he saw patterns that tied into his incest experience. The fact that he never pushed ahead to take over a company was his unconscious response to guilt about replacing the company father-figure – the boss.

Jackson was fortunate in that he had the courage and intelligence to seek treatment. Many victims suffer symptoms similar to his without ever doing anything about them. Many of these men were victims of the less overt forms of incest, yet their symptoms are no less severe. This is what makes mother–son incest so difficult to diagnose in many cases, for neither the mother nor the son may know that anything sexual occurred. It is because the borderlines of mother–son incest are so vague that every parent should know something about it.

Some activities that seem perfectly innocent on the surface – such as allowing a son to sleep in his mother's bed – can lead to later problems in socio-sexual development. Such nonsexual incest traumas are called pseudo-incest, and, as I have pointed out, can be just as damaging as true incest. Because of this the parental bed should not become an habitual sleeping place for a child of either sex, nor should sleeping privileges be granted as a special treat. A child should sleep in his mother's (or father's) bed only in an 'emergency' – say, during a frightening storm, or when the child is sick and needs constant tending.

However, aside from this pronouncement, I shy away from setting guidelines about how old a son should be before he bathes himself, dresses himself, or the like. Every mother–son relationship is unique, and every mother and son have different needs. There are no rules to follow to avoid pseudo-incest; instead, avoidance is a matter of exercising common sense and good judgement. If a ten-year-old boy asks his mother to scrub his back in the bath, he is probably making an innocent request. If he asks her to bathe him he is after more than cleanliness, and she should remind him gently that he is old enough to wash himself. The difference between a reasonable activity and one that stems from ulterior motives usually requires only a moment's consideration to determine.

A mother should not worry about incest in her everyday interaction with her son. Just as harmful as pseudo- or actual incest is emotional neglect as a reaction against incest fears. If a mother concentrates on raising her son to be self-confident and independent, she will inherently protect against incest.

8 · SIBLING INCEST

Siblings are generally so inclined to experiment sexually that some experts estimate that at least casual sibling sexual contact occurs in nine out of ten families with more than one child. Sibling incest is by far the most widespread form of incest, though it often goes unreported, even when discovered.

Under certain very specific circumstances sibling incest may not be a traumatic, or even unpleasant, experience. If the children are young and approximately the same age, if there is no betrayal of trust between them, if the sexual play is the result of their natural curiosity and exploration, and if the children are not traumatized by disapproving adults who stumble upon them during sex play, sibling sexual contact can be just another part of growing up. In most such cases both partners are sexually naïve. The game of show-me-yours-and-I'll-show-you-mine is older than civilization, and between young siblings of approximately the same age it is usually harmless.

When these circumstances are not ideal, however, a sibling victim can be as severely traumatized as any victim of an adult aggressor. These are the victims that I see in my practice. Most often they are female victims of an older brother who has taken advantage of their sexual naïveté to satisfy his sexual cravings or to cope with various unconscious conflicts. The greater the age difference between siblings the more violent the incest tends to be. And, generally, the more violent the sibling incest the more destructive the trauma. Also the larger the age difference between siblings the stronger the role of the older sibling as an authority figure, and thus the greater the betrayal of trust.

To understand sibling incest we must realize that each variation in the ages and sexes of the participants – older brother–younger sister, older sister–younger brother, heterosexual sex between siblings of the same age, homosexual sex between siblings of the same age, and homosexual sex between siblings of differing ages – has unique dynamics. Though I will discuss briefly the characteristics of these variations I will focus in this chapter on the most common type of sibling incest – older brother–younger sister.

OLDER BROTHER–YOUNGER SISTER

There are two general scenarios that older brother–younger sister incest usually follows. In the first there is only a few years' difference between the siblings, and the brother, generally around puberty, uses his sister as a sexual guinea pig. Since the younger sister is usually naïve, and often views the sexuality as a game, this scenario is often more damaging to the aggressor than to the victim. He may suffer substantial guilt over having taken advantage of his sister's affection and trust.

The second circumstance involves an aggressor who is a number of years older than his sister, and sexually abuses her – often violently – for complex psychological reasons that are only in part sexually motivated. I will present a case to illustrate each type.

Eric and Lucy Tobson

The first case, of Eric and Lucy Tobson, came to my attention by accident. I met twenty-one-year-old Lucy while waiting for a dental appointment. When I mentioned that I was working on this book she suggested that we meet for coffee after our respective checkups, and she would tell me about her incestuous experience.

She later told me of a two-year relationship with her brother, involving only minimal sexual contact. She seemed to have no feelings of guilt or regret about the relationship. Her story was especially valuable to my research because she told me I might also interview her brother. This was a rare opportunity, because it is usually difficult to contact more than one participant in long-past incest cases.

I eventually set up an interview with Eric in New York. When I arrived I expected to find an amiable young man with much the same casual attitude toward the incest as his sister had shown. I was surprised to find him anxious and suspicious, more so than any other person I interviewed for this book.

Eric, twenty-four years old, is in his second year of medical school and plans to be a psychiatrist. He is a handsome young man of medium height, brown hair, and brown eyes that he has a habit of averting when he speaks. The first thing he did when I entered his apartment was to type up a contract for me to sign, ensuring that I would write nothing that would reveal his identity. Then he refused to let me tape record our session. He was afraid that if it became known that he was the aggressor in this case, his future career would be ruined. I assured him that I would be discreet, and that he had done nothing so evil that it would have any effect on his career even if I were to identify him by name in this book. Reluctantly he began his story, and only by continual encouragement did I manage to get him to finish it.

Eric was raised in a family of four children – three brothers and Lucy. She is four years younger than he. They lived in Massachusetts, where their father was a successful veterinarian. The family lived very comfortably, but home life was defined by a self-absorbed, perfectionist father who never showed emotion to either his children or his wife. Eric described him as being 'emotionally absent from home, interested only in his work, golf, and tennis. He was always making me feel guilty about something – my grades, or not cleaning up my room. It was the kind of house where you were walking around on eggshells all the time. When my father was down – which was often – the whole house was down. When he was in a good mood, though, life was a party.'

Eric's next oldest brother was extremely intelligent, and Eric was made to feel inferior. To reap some of the attention his parents heaped on his brother Eric became very helpful around the house, always doing extra chores and trying to be good. Even so his father only criticized him.

Eric had once felt close to his mother when he was small, but when he was five years old, his 'genius' brother, whom he idolized, told him that he shouldn't be so 'kissy' with his mother. Taking this advice to heart Eric began rejecting her affection, and soon their relationship became distant.

His relationship with his little sister was always one of mutually loving antagonism. As is natural for young siblings they were jealous of each other's possessions and affections, and often fought, but just as often played peacefully.

As Eric entered puberty – he was about twelve, Lucy was eight – and became more sexually driven and sophisticated he developed a game in which he and Lucy would compete for kisses by throwing ping-pong balls into a waste-basket. If he won she would kiss him; if she won she wouldn't have to. (Lucy didn't see the sense in kissing.) Eventually these stakes began to bore him, so he developed a new game called Stowaway. In this game they would be stowaways in the dark hold of a ship (his closet), and would cling to each other as the ship rocked in the waves.

She would always lie on the bottom, and he would simulate intercourse through their clothes. As the game progressed they began taking off their clothes – with the exception of their underwear. He began imposing on her to play Stowaway with him while they were watching television, and he would lie on top of her in the family den. She would keep her eyes glued to the TV, apparently unaware that her brother was sexually aroused.

'I remember one day when I talked Lucy into taking off all our clothes,' says Eric, 'but she didn't want to touch me. We just lay there side by side, naked on the bed. I was tremendously aroused; she developed very early into a very attractive girl. I guess she was about nine, and I was thirteen. I remember I just barely touched my penis to her leg and I ejaculated. It was the first time I had ever ejaculated, and I was pretty excited about it. She had been facing the other direction, so she didn't know what had happened. I just got up and went into my room. She came in a few minutes later and accused me of peeing in her bed. I got a little paranoid, thinking that maybe she would get pregnant or something.

'I decided to tell my mother about it and maybe she could help me stop playing with Lucy, because it had gotten beyond my control. But when I went downstairs to find her she had already gone to sleep. By the next morning I had changed my mind. Lucy and I never stripped completely again, but I almost always ejaculated after that when we played Stowaway.

'A couple of months later we were playing Stowaway in my closet, and my mother came knocking on my door for Lucy. She wanted to know why my door was locked. I threw on my clothes and opened the door, and she came in and started looking around. Then she opened the closet, and there was Lucy lying on the floor with nothing on but her panties.

'I didn't know what was going to happen. My mother just told me to stay in my room and took Lucy to hers. I guess she grilled her to find out how far we had gone, but Lucy never really knew we were doing anything, so my mother didn't get much out of her. Meanwhile I sat there wondering what was going to happen to me, feeling incredibly guilty. I was actually never punished. She just told me not to do it again. My father knew about it, but he didn't get involved, didn't say a word.

'The relationship started up again soon after that because I couldn't control it. I was surprised that I was never more severely punished for it, but it wouldn't have mattered anyway. I remember one of the last times we ever did anything was when the family took a trip to New York. I was fourteen and Lucy was ten. We shared a room, and that night we began touching each other's bodies. I touched her breasts, and she touched my genitals – or at least she got close, I don't remember. Then it just ended. I guess I felt too guilty about it. Once she got old enough to know what was going on it became embarrassing for me.

'I became very touchy about it. Maybe three or four times a year since then, at the dinner table, my mother would make some little crack or joke about Stowaway, and I'd get so angry I'd have to leave the table. It wasn't until I went into therapy two years ago that I began to be able to handle it.'

Though the sexual experimentation between Eric and Lucy began innocently enough it progressed to the point where Eric realized he could not stop it. He felt a compulsion to repeat the incest, even after they had been caught at it. This mysterious compulsion is found in all forms of incest. Eric was virtually enslaved by his incestuous needs. Perhaps after his brother made him feel guilty for being too 'kissy' with his mother he projected his Oedipal yearnings from his mother to Lucy, adding a powerful incentive for him to act on the sexual urges of his puberty. Whatever the motivation Eric could not control himself. His guilt was so excruciating that he considered confessing to his mother, yet he could not bring himself to refrain from his incestuous games.

In the end it was Lucy who actually ended the relationship, not by any conscious action, but by outgrowing the innocence that allowed Eric to use her with impunity as a sexual plaything. This, in itself, might not have been enough to overcome Eric's compulsion, but it coincided with that time in his life when his peers were beginning to become sexually active, so he managed to transfer his needs to girls in his peer group.

This case is typical of the type of incest situation that some theorists insist results in no harm to either sibling. Yet Eric is clearly laboring under tremendous guilt. Throughout the interview, whenever Eric mentioned anything specific – the number of siblings in the family, the profession of his father, the fact that his brother was a genius – he would stop and ask that I disguise the fact in my notes. The remotest connections worried him. With each fact I had to reassure him that his anonymity would not be jeopardized.

It fascinated me that he could have so much anxiety over what seemed to me an extremely innocent string of episodes that many therapists would not even classify as incestuous. Even the victim felt that she had suffered no real harm. Eric's parents considered his activities hardly worthy of reprimand. Still he feared that even the vaguest reference that could identify him with the case would ruin his future. There is obviously something larger than Stowaway at work here. Eric is a victim of the incest taboo. Unconsciously he may feel he has violated a law of nature in so perverse a way that he can never recover from the shame.

He is only now beginning to pull out of this emotional rut after two years of analysis. Surely the coldness of his father contributed to his problems, but he attributes the bulk of his psychological difficulties to the incest.

I doubt that most older brother–younger sister incest is as innocent as many modern theorists would have us believe. Older siblings, like Eric, often feel a burdensome responsibility for having taken advantage of their younger sisters. Such guilt follows people throughout their lives, making them feel uneasy around women, distrustful of their own self-control, and unsure of their roles in social situations. These men often become overly shy, and in extreme cases, impotent from guilt. They carry always the image of their innocent, young sisters unknowingly surrendering themselves to the older brothers they trust. They carry always the knowledge of having violated that trust.

The second type of older-brother aggressor, several years older than his younger sister, tends to be a disturbed individual *before* the incest begins. He is like the father-aggressor who uses incest as a means of trying to cope with unconscious needs and conflicts. This older brother is usually intimidated by women, often because of a cold domineering mother. He finds his little sister's passivity nonthreatening. Just as some incestuous fathers turn their daughters into symbolic mothers the incestuous brother may abuse his little sister as a means of acting out his aggression toward *his* mother. Because of the aggressor's hostility this form of incest is often violent. The older brother is usually much larger and stronger than his younger sister, and his abuse often takes the form of forcible rape.

As in father–daughter incest the older brother–younger sister household is usually an unhappy, uncommunicative one. The older brother is often a father figure to his sister, not only by virtue of his age, but because the domineering mother often causes her husband to withdraw from the family, to become emotionally isolated, so the brother fills his role as disciplinarian of the younger children. The trust that is betrayed here is very close to that of father–daughter incest. Even Oedipal attractions may be involved, as the sister may transfer her Oedipal attraction from her father to her fatherlike brother.

In the case that follows the mother played a silent partner role as if it were a case of father–daughter incest. She pushed her daughter into the incestuous relationship, seemingly in an unconscious effort to deal with her own Oedipal attraction to her son.

Leslie Bogen

Leslie Bogen is a tall woman in her mid-forties, with pale red hair cut close to her head. She is not an attractive woman, for her face is etched with harsh lines that reflect a life of misery. She resembles one of those turn-of-the-century photographs of a weathered Indian squaw – in fact her father was a full-blooded Iroquois. Her body is hard and lean, almost masculine. She speaks with very little inflection in a deep voice clearly affected by her chain smoking.

I first met Leslie when she was admitted to the hospital after a suicide attempt. Her lesbian lover had left her after a number of years of living together, and Leslie had fallen into a deep depression from which death seemed her only escape.

Born the youngest of six children in a struggling middle-class family in Portland, Oregon, Leslie always felt unwanted: 'My mother always treated me worse than my brothers and sisters. It was hell. She just didn't want me. She was forty-five when I was born, so I'm sure I was a burden to her. She used to beat me all the time.

'She was always arguing with my father. He would try to leave the house and she'd strike him. He'd never hit her back because he was a good man, a fine-looking man – black-haired, brown-eyed, Indian – handsome as hell.

My mother spent all her time keeping him under her thumb. It's not that he played around – he never had time for that. He was too busy working to support his six kids. He was a good man. The only thing wrong with him was that he was henpecked.

'So he'd go off to work and my mother would proceed to pick on me. I don't know why – she just hated for me to breathe. She had a stick about a yard long, with the edges split about halfway up, that she used to whip me with. Then she'd patch me up – she was a nurse. When I was fourteen I threatened to kill myself if she ever beat me again; I figured I'd be better off dead than beaten half to death. You can see why I didn't think it would do me much good to tell her when my brother raped me. He was her favorite.

'We lived in a big house that my father had built with his own hands. My bedroom was way up in the attic. It was dark and stuffy up there, and I was afraid because my brother told me there were "niggers" up there who would get me. So one night my mother told me to go to bed and I cried because my brother had been scaring me, so she told me to get into his bed and sleep with him. I had done this many times, it was no big deal, so I went in and went to sleep. I was five at the time and he was close to sixteen.

'When he came in that night he raped me. It hurt like hell. I felt scared. When it was over I cried. He told me not to tell anybody or he'd kill me. It scared me bad.

'The next time it happened I didn't want to get in his bed, but I was so scared of my room that I kept crying, so my mother made me get in bed with him. I told my mother I didn't want to, but she told me if I didn't she'd beat my hide.

'So that night he did it again. I don't know how many times it happened after that. It just kept happening. My mother would make me get in bed with him, and then he'd rape me. I remember feeling sticky afterwards, and it hurt so bad. He'd wipe me off with a towel.

'Finally I couldn't take it anymore, so I told my mother I wasn't afraid anymore and would sleep in my own bed. I could hardly sleep I was so afraid of that room, but I did it anyway. He never dared try to rape me again because if we weren't in his bed he could be caught.

'After that I withdrew a lot. I never had a lot of friends, because I was afraid to bring any home, but after my brother raped me I couldn't face anyone. I was ashamed. I didn't understand what he was doing to me, but I knew it was wrong because it hurt and because he told me not to tell.

'It was hell living with him for years in that house. I'd just avoid him as much as possible. Finally he moved out, and I've only seen him twice since then.

'The first time was about fifteen years ago when I went over to his house to see his wife and baby. I came walking in and he said, "Here comes my sister, built like a Belgian stud-horse," and I just couldn't take it. I always wanted to let him have it so I just beat him into the ground. He was bigger than I was, but I had the advantage because I got him down first. I kicked him where it hurt – in the balls. Oh, that made me feel great. I stomped him with my feet, broke his nose, beat him half to death. I embarrassed him so bad in front of his neighbors that he had to move.

'But he got even when my sister died about four years ago. That was the last time I saw him. I went to the funeral and he beat me up. My mother was standing right there. My face was a bloody mess. I didn't fight back, but boy did I open my big mouth. I said, "Mother, I want you to take a good look at your child molester. He raped me again and again when I was little, but I was always afraid to tell you." She didn't say a word, she just stood there. That was the first time I ever told anybody about it. She wouldn't let him in her home for a few years, but now I think she's letting him back in. After all, she's ninety-three and he was always her favorite.'

Leslie has been married three times, and she has three children, all from her second marriage. Her second husband was the only man – aside from her brother – she has ever slept with.

'I married the first one,' she recalls, 'and I wouldn't go to bed with him. I was seventeen-and-a-half. My mother had a job offer, and she couldn't take me with her, so she said either I got married or she would send me to a detention home. She was a bigwig in the probation department at the time, so she could have done it. Naturally I decided to get married. Fortunately I had my period on our wedding night, and after that I went to live with my aunt. I wouldn't stay with him. That marriage lasted about three months.

'Then I married John, and we were married for a couple of years before my little boy was born. Again I got married because of my mother's threats. Sleeping with him was horrible. It brought back memories of my brother. And I had been going with a girl at that time, which is what made my mother angry.

'During the whole marriage I was seeing women on the side. That's why we got divorced. He told my mother about my lesbian relationships, and she had my kids taken away. I worked two jobs for several years to save money for an attorney to get my children back, but it didn't do any good.

'I finally married a gay boy to get my children back. But he and I never lived together. I raised those kids with my lover. They're good kids.

'The woman who helped me raise them is named Francine. I supported her most of the time, and she lived with me for fifteen years. But then we split up because she'd been stepping out on me. Then I met Bette. We lived together six years and then she split on me. That's what brought on this hospitalization.'

Leslie believes she was born with 'homosexual tendencies,' but I think her homosexuality is a defensive flight from men. This type of reaction to incest is not the norm, but neither is it unusual. Aside from the incest the only heterosexual sexual relationship she has ever had revolted her because 'it brought back memories of my brother.' Even if her homosexual tendencies did form before her brother raped her the incest certainly touched them off. Homosexual reactions to incest are much more common in mother–son cases and, to a lesser extent, father–son cases than they are in sibling cases, however.

In lesbian relationships Leslie plays the part of the male – called the 'butch.' Her relationships are very clearly defined in terms of who is dominant and who is not – just as the relationships in her family were. She has always been a domineering woman, like her mother, and has ultimately driven her lovers away because she has not allowed herself to open up emotionally. She became a cold, demanding woman, incapable of the kind of tenderness that is required to sustain a relationship after the initial sexual passion has diminished.

Clearly Leslie was still carrying her incest trauma before her last hospitalization. When she was domineering, when she was tough, she was symbolically dominating her brother, she was gaining control of a situation that had been beyond her control during the critical moments four decades before. When she was cruel and bitter she was once again kicking her brother where it hurt. Yet despite her hatred of her brother, despite her accusations, she still felt guilty about the incest. She had a terrible self-image and a great capacity for depression. When she entered the hospital she was diagnosed not only as suicidal, but as homicidal. She wanted to kill both herself and her abandoning lover.

I found Leslie to be a difficult patient. She refused to open up to me just as she had been refusing to open up to anyone throughout her life. For forty years she had been internalizing all her hurts and her joys, and she felt threatened by the possibility of finally revealing them.

'How do I know you won't hurt me?' she asked. 'What for?' I answered. 'You're doing a better job of hurting yourself than I could ever do. At least by trusting me you'd give yourself a chance.'

The day she finally revealed her incest to the group she wept. She told us we were the first people ever to see her cry. She left the hospital after three months of treatment, still somewhat depressed, yet committed to picking up the pieces and reassembling her life.

OLDER SISTER–YOUNGER BROTHER

Just as older brother–younger sister incest has parallels to father–daughter incest, older sister–younger brother incest is similar in many respects to mother–son incest. The boy's symptoms are the same – insecurity, guilt, inability to relate to women, and sometimes impotence. And many of the dynamics are similar. For example the physiological demand that the boy maintain an erection causes these relationships to be characterized by some tenderness. Thus as in mother–son incest the victim doesn't understand that he has been victimized. Instead he suffers guilt because he feels he has been an active accomplice. His guilt may later make him uneasy around women, all of whom will remind him of his sister.

In a 1976 *Redbook* article Masters and Johnson cited two cases of older sister–younger brother incest, both involving broken homes with absent fathers – just as in the mother–son scenario. In one case the sister was seven years older than her brother, and in the other case, ten years older. Both victims became impotent when they eventually tried to have sexual relationships with peers.

'In both cases it was the boy who had fought free of the all consuming, semimaternal relationship,' Masters and Johnson wrote. 'There was no withdrawal of sexual demands by the older sister.'

An older sister usually turns sexually to a younger brother because she feels inadequate and threatened in peer relationships. Her younger brother is an undemanding sexual partner. She grows to depend on him, and will not let him go. She becomes maternal and overprotective, like the mother–son aggressor.

This semimaternal aspect is of key importance, for it signals a transfer of Oedipal attractions. The victim lives out his Oedipal fantasies for his mother with his sister. When he attempts to have intercourse later in life his partner reminds him of his sister, with whom making love was symbolic of having sex with his mother. As a defense against this unconscious chain of deep-seated guilts the victim becomes impotent and avoids women.

HOMOSEXUAL SIBLING INCEST

In young siblings – say, up to age seven – homosexual contact does not necessarily imply homosexual attraction. Body exploration is natural, and often without a sexual context. But as children become aware of sexuality, homosexual incest between siblings can often signal a homosexual preference. Sibling incest is unlikely to *lead* to such a preference, however – more often the homosexual preference leads to the incest.

As in heterosexual sibling incest the greater the age difference between the participants in homosexual sibling incest the greater the chance that the aggressor will use violence to force himself or herself on the victim. And, generally, the greater the force the greater the trauma.

I reviewed a case of violent homosexual sibling incest last year, from police files, in which a fourteen-year-old boy was picked up for prostitution. He was not arrested, because under California law anyone under sixteen picked up for a sex offense is considered a victim rather than a perpetrator. But he was detained until his parents could be notified. The boy spoke freely with police officers, and admitted that he had performed anal and oral intercourse with over one hundred men. When he was asked how he became involved in sexual activities he said that his two older brothers – sixteen and eighteen – had raped him. This abuse apparently affected the boy harshly, destroying his self-respect and leading to his self-degrading life as a 'chicken,' a boy prostitute.

Victims of homosexual incest typically suffer deep depresion, self-loathing, both homosexual and heterosexual sexual problems, and confusion over their sexual identity.

DISCOVERING INCESTUOUS SIBLINGS

A parent's typical reactions to discovering young siblings engaged in sexual play are anger, shame, accusations, and sometimes violence. Such reactions are always inappropriate, and usually harmful. Recriminations can, in themselves, create guilt and inhibitions that the siblings may carry for the rest of their lives. Threats or beatings are seldom as effective in dissuading siblings from further sexual transgressions as a heart-to-heart talk about the role of sex in healthy human relationships. Young children often have no idea of what they are doing when they engage in sexual activities. Their being discovered offers a parent an ideal context within which to explain the basics of reproduction, sexuality, and love. It is evident from the fact that the siblings are engaged in sexual play that they are curious about sex, and within limits, if they are old enough to experiment with sex, they are old enough to understand it.

Older children, on the other hand, generally know very well what they are doing when they engage in sexual activities, and an aggressive reaction from parents may serve merely to make them stealthier. If older siblings persist in their sexual contact, or if one of the siblings is considerably older than the other (whether they persist or not), professional psychological counseling is usually necessary to help straighten out their confusion and steer them toward appropriate peer relationships.

This chapter is not intended to make parents fearful that their children will engage in incest, and it is certainly not intended to encourage parents to separate siblings or forbid physical contact between them. Aside from the confusion over the unwarranted punishment that the siblings will feel, and the resentment they will feel toward their parents if such restrictions are imposed, research has shown that physical separation of siblings while they are young may *promote* incest when they grow older. According to British sociologist J. R. Fox: 'The more intensive the bodily interaction between opposite-sex children during sexual immaturity, the more likely the possibility that they will voluntarily abstain from sexual relations with each other after puberty.' In other words, if siblings participate in nonsexual physical contact games when they are young, there will be less 'mystery' in touching when they grow older. Later physical contact will not be alluring, it will be boring – old hat.

The most effective way for a parent to guard against sibling incest is to simply maintain an open, honest relationship with the children. If one sibling sexually approaches another, either child should feel free to talk to his or her parents about the incident, without fearing punishment or verbal abuse. This may entail suppression of instinctive anger or indignation on the part of some parents, but the effort is well worth the results.

Sibling incest is a family problem, and it tends to become a serious problem in those families where an abused child has no one to turn to for help. If children can speak openly about anything with their parents, without fear, casual sexual experimentation will almost certainly not develop into habitual incestuous abuse. Like most other forms of incest sibling incest cannot thrive without the shield of secrecy.

9 · GRANDFATHER–GRANDDAUGHTER INCEST

There is something about the image of the gentle, understanding, loving grandfather with his adorable, Shirley Templish granddaughter on his knee that epitomizes the All-American Family. Incest seems particularly out of place in this loving scene, for grandfathers are traditionally considered harmless old men, and the age difference between their granddaughters and them would appear to make the sexual contact absurd. But there is a skeleton in the closet of the All-American family – grandfather–granddaughter incest – which accounts for as many as 10 percent of my cases.

Like most other forms of incest grandfather–granddaughter incest has gone unchronicled in both professional and lay periodicals. Nothing has been written on it, no research has been done on it, and from talks with colleagues I gather that very little is understood about it. So my analysis, though based on fairly extensive case material of my own, is necessarily speculative.

There are generally two types of grandfather aggressors: relatively young men, say in their forties and fifties, and older men who may have begun to feel the physical deterioration of age.

THE YOUNG GRANDFATHER

In cases of younger grandfather-aggressors there are many parallels with father–daughter incest. For one thing the victims generally suffer the same type of guilt – feelings of responsibility for the incest, competitiveness with the aggressor's wife, and sometimes feelings of having enjoyed the incestuous caresses. Also this type of incest usually occurs in families that have suffered an emotional breakdown between the grandfather and his wife. If the granddaughter is living with her grandparents, this breakdown can be identical to the typical father–daughter family breakdown.

The incestuous grandfather's attraction for his granddaughter is often the same attraction that the father-aggressor feels for his daughter. In fact the grandfather may abuse his granddaughter as a means of acting out his incestuous desires for his daughter – the victim's mother. Though he is attracted to his daughter he may be unable to breach that particular incest taboo. So he projects his attraction onto his granddaughter. By removing the incest by one generation he somehow perceives the taboo as less powerful.

Finally the victim's grandmother often assumes a typical silent partner role. The following case illustrates many of these dynamics.

Cass Dalton

I first began treating Cass Dalton when she entered one of my outpatient groups seeking treatment of chronic migraine headaches. She was twenty-five, very attractive, alert, friendly, and outgoing. At first glance – aside from the headaches – she exhibited none of the classic symptoms of incest.

As she began telling her story to the group she seemed nervous, as if she were hiding something. It didn't take much encouragement to get the secret out – her grandfather had molested her regularly for about two years from the time she was nine years old.

'He would manhandle me,' she said, 'and I remember bleeding from him getting so carried away with touching me and feeling me. He didn't have any teeth and he would French-kiss me – I wouldn't throw up or anything, but I would feel ill.

'I never saw my grandparents hug or kiss. My grandmother probably wouldn't give him anything [sexually]. She used to be in the hospital a lot and I was living with them at the time because my parents were separated. When I finished my chores I would stay outside the house a lot, rather than be alone with my grandfather, but he never failed to get me. Even when my grandmother was around we would all go to the store and she would go shopping while I'd be stuck in the car with him. He would say, "Come here," and there was nothing I could do. I was scared to death. He was always touching me and wanting to kiss me.

'I've been paying men back ever since. I'll get a man to like me – it's really easy to get men to fall in love with me and I attract the kind who want to settle down – then I'll find his weakness and dig at it. I'll really dig deep and I'll hurt him as much as I can. I don't do it intentionally. Until he falls in love with me I'll play to his good side, but once he falls for me I just turn a cold shoulder. I think it's my way of punishing men for what my grandfather did.'

Her grandmother's frequent hospitalizations and emotional isolation from Cass's grandfather set up the incest situation in the classic pattern of the silent partner in father–daughter cases. Because her grandmother was so often bedridden Cass assumed many of the household duties, moving into the maternal role. Her grandmother's emotional withdrawal helped transform that role into a sexual one.

Cass's grandfather was only in his late forties, just a few years older than the average incestuous father. For Cass, who lived with her grandparents, he had, in fact, assumed a paternal role – he was the household authority figure, the breadwinner, the disciplinarian. Cass related to him as a father to such an extent that the added generation between aggressor and victim in this case seems almost incidental – the dynamics are virtually identical to those of father–daughter incest.

Cass's symptoms, too, were typical of those found in father–daughter cases. Not only is she unable to trust a man, but she punishes herself by not allowing herself to enjoy a fulfilling relationship with a man. These are problems she is still working on, though she has managed through therapy to gain a good measure of self-confidence and self-respect – qualities that she had previously lacked.

The parallels between Cass's situation and father–daughter incest were promoted by the fact that her grandparents were raising her in their home, as if she were their own child. In the second type of grandfather–granddaughter incest this situation is often reversed – the grandfather often comes to live in his child's home. This fosters an entirely different set of dynamics, which are unique to this pattern of incest.

THE OUT-TO-PASTURE GRANDFATHER

Typically the older incestuous grandfather is a victim of society's assumption that aging and deterioration are one. He is often 'put out to pasture' in forced retirement. His identity and self-respect, which are often closely tied to a career, now flounder. Whether he is growing senile or not his family treats him as if he were. With little to fill his time he becomes bored and cranky. Because of this his relationship with his child begins to deteriorate, especially if he is living with him or her. He may resent his family because of his dependence on them. This resentment and general helplessness drives him closer to his granddaughter, for she is not yet strong enough to consider him weak. She is not aware of his fragility. She feeds his ego, making him feel strong, young again. He yearns to re-experience the vigor of his youth. He is fighting for his identity, his manhood, but he has no means of proving it anymore – except one. His penis.

At his age sexual partners are often hard to find, and even if he could find an adult partner he would most likely suffer tremendous performance anxiety. With his young granddaughter he doesn't have to worry about adult sexual expectations, about performing up to par. He can assert his manhood – and thereby recapture his youth – by using his penis, yet his performance won't be judged. So, often consigned to the role of babysitter, he finds ample opportunities to develop sexual activities with his granddaughter.

The victim of an incestuous grandfather is in danger of suffering a particularly devastating trauma. If her grandfather should happen to die during the course of an incestuous relationship she may feel responsible for his death. She may feel to blame for having overexcited her grandfather or, if she had been avoiding his advances, she may feel that in depriving him of his sexual gratification she has somehow contributed to his death. While such reasoning is unrealistic a child's fantasy world has little to do with logic. I have heard such stories at times from patients.

The following is a particularly dramatic example of how death can play a key role in the incest trauma.

Lindsay Morrow

I first heard of this case from an old friend and colleague, Dr Paul Hendershaw. We were talking late one night about this book, and he mentioned a few details of the case that were so compelling I persuaded him to dig out his case notes and give me a complete account. For the next two hours he recreated the case as if it were a psychological detective story, and that is how I have chosen to present it.

The story opens in Upper Arlington, a suburb of Columbus, Ohio, in the winter of 1972. Hendershaw was awakened in the middle of the night by the telephone.

'Dr Hendershaw?' The man sounded scared, concerned. 'My name is Morrow. John Morrow.' In the background Hendershaw heard sounds of struggle and shouting. Then he heard a chilling, low-pitched, raspy voice. It was spewing continuous obscenities. Occasionally it would break into lewd song. Hendershaw tried to concentrate on what Morrow was telling him, but that voice kept gripping his attention. A vision of Regan, the little girl possessed by the devil in *The Exorcist*, forced itself upon him. It sounded like the same voice.

'Doctor, we need your help,' Morrow was saying. 'My wife is going crazy – I don't know how else to describe it. She's ... my brother's here, and we're both pretty big men, but we can barely control her. She's screaming and throwing things around ...'

Hendershaw instructed Morrow to somehow get his wife to a nearby psychiatric hospital where Hendershaw would meet them. As he dressed he kept hearing that voice.

When Hendershaw reached the hospital he found two athletic-looking men, both over six feet tall, seated on either side of a petite blonde, barely five feet tall, and probably not weighing much more than a hundred pounds. He tried to correlate this slightly disheveled, well-dressed, blue-eyed woman with the harsh, vulgar voice he had heard over the phone, but the two images would not blend.

One of the men introduced himself as John Morrow, then presented his wife Lindsay, and his brother Fred. Lindsay sat leaning back, looking as if she had missed a night's sleep. Her eyes were red, one of her fingers was bandaged, and she had a fresh bruise on her right forearm. Other than that Hendershaw noticed nothing unusual about her. In her dark-blue woolen suit and carefully layered shoulder-length hairdo she struck him as a typical junior-leaguer, the model active young wife.

He asked her to tell him what had happened.

'I ... I don't remember,' she said. 'I must have had a little too much to drink. Whatever it was it couldn't have been as bad as they say.' She laughed lightly, as if to imply that her husband was blowing a minor incident out of proportion. Hendershaw began to believe her. Her voice was soft, gentle – he must have misheard that demonic voice in the background.

'She wasn't drunk,' said Morrow. 'She only had two glasses of sherry, which is not unusual for her. I've never seen her drunk. We were just sitting, talking, when some sort of terrible grimace came over her face. Then all of a sudden she started swearing and singing these dirty songs. And her voice . . . I can't even describe it. It was like another person's – like a man's voice. She started throwing things – plates, ashtrays, glasses, books, whatever she could lay her hands on. I didn't know what to do so I called my doctor. He referred me to you.'

'Had she taken any drugs?' Hendershaw asked. 'Anything at all?'

'No. Not a thing.'

'Has she ever had any similar attacks before? Or have you noticed anything in her behavior lately that's at all out of the ordinary?'

'No.'

Hendershaw took down the woman's medical and family histories, but found nothing unusual. She was twenty-eight years old, and had come from a New Haven, Connecticut, working-class family. Her father had been a construction worker; he died when she was in her teens. She was the youngest of five children, the next youngest being six years older than she, so she was always 'the baby.' Hers was a loving family, with no history of physical abuse or unusual problems.

When Lindsay was six her maternal grandfather, a former merchant marine, who had been living with the family for several years, died of cancer. Lindsay took this death very hard, and developed recurring nightmares and unusual fears. She not only feared the dark, but was afraid of specific places in the house – an alcove at the top of the stairs, her grandfather's room, and her closet. For several years she would ask her sisters to get her clothes from the closet or to turn lights on for her.

Lindsay always did well in school, and had gone on to college from high school, studying to be a librarian. But when she was twenty her mother died and Lindsay decided to leave school and move to Columbus, where her best friend had moved. There she trained to be a legal secretary and went to work for John Morrow's law firm.

Within a year she and Morrow were married. They moved into a beautiful home in Upper Arlington — not far from Hendershaw's house — and Lindsay became active in civic activities. She was the perfect hostess, the perfect guest, the perfect organizer, the perfect wife. At night she would become the perfect seductress, and John never realized that she faked her orgasms.

After about three years of marriage the Morrows decided to have a baby. About a month after their decision Lindsay had the attack that led her to Hendershaw.

The day after the attack Lindsay looked fresh and pretty when she appeared at Hendershaw's office door. She was cheerful and a bit apologetic for having roused him from his bed the night before. 'My husband makes mountains of molehills,' she said.

Over the next month Hendershaw saw her three times a week, and every time she came she impressed him as being 'the perfect psychiatric patient.' In retrospect he realized she had been too perfect. Each time a crisis would come up she would resolve it. Her stories were all very pat, almost rehearsed. There seemed to be nothing there to give Hendershaw any clues about the mysterious attack, about the voice he had overheard on the telephone.

He sent her to a neurologist for testing to rule out any possible physiological disorders that might have explained her unusual actions.

Hendershaw also considered the possibility of acute alcohol intolerance, a rare condition in which just a small amount of alcohol can send a person into a wild rage. But he decided that since she had never shown radical reactions to alcohol before this was an unlikely possibility.

Therapy sessions continued to be uneventful. Then, a month after the first attack, Hendershaw received another middle-of-the-night phone call. Another attack. Morrow was alone with his wife this time, so Hendershaw summoned an ambulance to help subdue Lindsay and get her to the hospital. Again when he arrived he found her slightly shaken but otherwise quite normal in appearance. As it had the first time her attack had subsided as soon as she had been wrestled into the vehicle that would take her to the hospital. It was an instantaneous transformation.

This time she had not been drinking, so that eliminated the possibility of acute alcohol intolerance. She had been upset that she had gotten her period, because she had been hoping she was pregnant. To stem her agitation she had borrowed a Seconal – a sleeping pill – from a neighbor. A half-hour later she suffered her second attack.

Hendershaw ordered an immediate battery of tests, hoping to pick up some abnormality in the wake of the attack. He gave her an EEG to check her brain waves, a Rorschach ink-blot test, another group of neurological tests, and more psychological and personality tests. Again the tests picked up nothing wrong physiologically, but she did show signs of psychological abnormalities. Hendershaw picked up signs of heavy repression indicating what is known as an 'as-if personality.'

'As-if' behavior is not limited to psychiatric patients; many people are adept at it. Like Lindsay they learn to walk, talk, act, and even feel *as if* they were healthy, spontaneous people, when actually they are repressing their real feelings. Sometimes they are so convincing that they fool their psychiatrists. Lindsay was clearly adept at this type of subtle role-playing – she had so easily adopted her upper-middle-class mannerisms. Hendershaw realized that she had also been acting during their therapy sessions, being the 'as-if' patient who was only slightly neurotic – disturbed enough to allay his suspicions, but not disturbed enough to require serious treatment or hospitalization. It was now obvious to him that she was repressing something extremely traumatic, so he decided to use medical hypnosis to break through her rigid defenses.

Two days later Hendershaw hypnotized her. When he was sure she was asleep he instructed her to open her eyes.

'Now think of a truck bearing down on you,' he said. 'The truck that you dreamed about last week. I want you to trace the roots of this particular dream. I want you to trace them back. Back to when you were a child. When I count to three that incident will trigger a memory from your childhood. One, two, three . . .'

'I remember coming home from school,' she said calmly.

'How old are you?'

'Six.'

'Go on.'

'My grandpa is in the house but no one else is there.'

'Go on.'

Her voice changed now to that of a little girl.

'No, Grandpa! Leave me alone!' She stood and began running toward the door.

'Sleep!' Hendershaw commanded.

She stopped in her tracks, hung her head, and closed her eyes.

'All right,' said Hendershaw. 'Come sit down on the couch and tell me about your grandpa.'

Still in her trance, she described a salty old man who would sing sea chanteys to her and take her on walks. She was his 'little princess.'

'Why were you running from your grandpa?' Hendershaw asked.

'He tried to get me,' she said.

'Why was he trying to get you?'

'I was running.'

'Why were you running?'

'I was scared.'

'Of what?'

'Grandpa.'

'Why?'

'I didn't want to play anymore.'

'Play what?'

'Little princess.'

She was becoming extremely agitated so Hendershaw decided to end the session.

'All right, Lindsay. Now it's December 19, 1976. I'm Dr Hendershaw and we're in my office. When I count to three I want you to wake up. You will remember as much of what you've said as you can handle, do you understand? If there is some memory that is too painful for you, you will not remember it when you wake up. One, two, three . . .'

In the next session Hendershaw used another of her dreams – this time of being pursued during wartime – as a hypnotic springboard into the past. Again she led him to her grandfather.

'Are you his little princess?' asked Hendershaw.

'Yes,' she replied in her six-year-old voice.

'Are you scared?'

She paused for a moment, as if paralyzed, then suddenly her face distorted into a macabre mask of pain and passion. As Hendershaw stared the voice he had first heard over the phone came out of her twisted mouth.

'You goddamn son-of-a-bitch whore, suck my cock,' she screamed in that unearthly rasp. 'I'm gonna get you, you shithole, and I'm gonna shove it up your ass!'

The words sounded so unreal that their lewd implications almost escaped him. She was no longer Lindsay. Her face was so contorted that she was unrecognizable. The words came out like meaningless cadences. Then she broke into a song, an obscene sailor's tale.

Suddenly Hendershaw realized who sat opposite him. This was not Lindsay he faced but her grandfather. These were his words, his dirty chanteys, his voice. She was carrying him inside her for some reason.

As Hendershaw listened, Lindsay lunged at him, clutching at his throat. He struggled with her momentarily, and was amazed at her strength. Then he commanded her to sleep.

Lindsay's story came out slowly over the next nine months. Whenever Hendershaw brought her out of hypnosis he would give her the same instructions about remembering only what she could handle. As she remembered more and more, her attacks became less frequent.

Her grandfather had come to live with the family after his wife had died. Lindsay was three at the time. She had taken an immediate liking to the crusty old man, and they soon became inseparable. Being the youngest child in the family she was often left with her grandfather while her mother went shopping and the older children were out playing. He would sit her on his knee, bounce her up and down, and call her his 'little princess.'

After a while this innocent affection became sexual, though Lindsay was too young to understand what was happening. Her grandfather would hug and kiss her and rub his hands all over her body. She enjoyed his caresses; they made her feel warm and loved.

'I am your prince,' he would say, 'and we will love each other forever.' This was heady stuff for a three-year-old going on four, and when he began French-kissing her she was captivated. Then his fingers began creeping into her panties. By the time she was four-and-a-half he was giving her lengthy vaginal massages, and had coaxed her into touching his penis occasionally. One day she masturbated him to a climax, frightening herself so that she burst into tears.

Soon after her fifth birthday he forced her to fellate him; she became nauseated. He began penetrating her vagina and her anus with objects — pencils, candles, whatever he had at hand. The sensual caresses that she had once enjoyed had evolved into activities that she found revolting and painful. She began avoiding her grandfather, but he would hide in her closet, or in the alcove at the top of the stairs, or around corners, and he would ambush her when she approached. If she told anyone, he would warn, he would get her at night while she slept.

As she walked home from school one day – she was six-and-a-half – she saw an ambulance parked in front of her house. She watched the attendants carry a stretcher from the house, and she knew that her grandfather was on it. That was the last time she ever saw him. He died a week later. His death was a great blow to her, despite her fear of him. She began to suffer attacks of depression and anger, and after a few years these evolved into multiple-personality episodes.

Lindsay learned quickly, when she left home for college, to anticipate when one of her episodes was about to occur. At first they would be triggered by anniversary events, such as the date her grandfather was taken to the hospital, the date he died, the date her mother died, and Easter – the Resurrection. But eventually she would have her attacks seemingly at random, two or three times a month. Still, she became aware of certain physical signs that warned her of coming attacks. Sometimes she would wake up in the morning and her throat would feel as if she had been screaming all night. Or sometimes her room would be in disarray, as if she had been throwing things in her sleep. At other times she felt stabbing pains in her vagina, or pounding in her head.

When one of these signs presaged an attack, she would find an excuse to go off by herself – to the country or a deserted warehouse – and let herself go for a bout of swearing and violence. In this way she hid her problem for two decades, until she was twenty-eight.

Lindsay remained a virgin until she married John. She was twenty-one. She was tense about sex because she feared that some physical damage her grandfather might have done would give away her past. When she made love with John her physical feelings mimicked the incomplete orgasms she had experienced as a child. She would have preorgasmic feelings, but then the orgasm would be aborted.

Throughout all this she never thought to seek help. She felt that her attacks were indelibly part of her life and that nothing could be done. It was not until she lost control in front of her husband that she ever saw a psychiatrist, and even then she resisted treatment until she was hypnotized.

It took her about a year to exorcize her grandfather – a year of remembering and understanding and crying and learning to cope – but finally she rid herself of him. She and John had their child – a boy – and she eventually became orgasmic. After three years she felt secure enough to leave therapy.

Lindsay's case is typical in many aspects – the grandfather reduced to living with his child and consigned to babysit, pleasure-guilt conflicts in the victim, 'as-if' role playing, guilt following the grandfather's death, and severe trauma.

The breakdown in the relationship between Lindsay's mother and grandfather was the result of understandable tensions resulting from his moving in with his daughter. To the mother this was both a physical and an emotional burden; to him it was a humiliation. He had come to live with his daughter because he could no longer take care of himself, a terrible admission of weakness and defeat for anyone. He was transformed from an independent retiree to a live-in babysitter. Isolated and fearing emasculation he was put in charge of a little girl who hugged him, kissed him, and sat on his knee. This rare physical contact delighted him. Eventually his pleasure became sexual, he lost control of his impulses, and the incest developed from there.

Lindsay, too, found pleasure in the sexual activities at first. Before his attentions became painful she felt flattered that he had chosen *her* as the object of his affections, rather than one of her older sisters, or even her mother. She appreciated being singled out (a pattern we see also in father–daughter cases). When the incest developed to the point where she no longer enjoyed it she became frightened, confused, and upset – but more than that she felt guilty, for she thought her initial acquiescence had caused his behavior. She started to avoid her grandfather, and this, too, aroused guilt.

She was miserable, but could turn to no one for help. She knew how much her mother loved the old man, and she understood that to expose his activities would hurt her mother very much – her grandfather had told her as much. Not only did she keep the relationship secret, but she had to act, when the family was around, *as if* she were not afraid of him. This is where she developed her extraordinary role-playing abilities. Instead of allowing her feelings to direct her, she figured out how a normal little girl would act around a normal grandfather, and when other people were about that is how she would act.

But her fears were paralyzing. She was afraid of all the places he would hide waiting for her – the top of the stairs, her closet, his room, etc. His threats to 'get' her at night caused her to fear the dark. These fears intensified greatly after he died. She was afraid he would come back to molest her, or to pay her back for what she saw as her role in his death.

She didn't understand why, but she felt that his death had been her fault. She had let him down. Her fears that he would return became obsessive. On the infrequent occasions that she went to church she could not look at the figure of Christ on the cross, for the Resurrection suggested to her that her grandfather might return. This, in turn, led to more guilt – for not wanting him to be resurrected.

She dealt with her conflicting feelings – love, fear, and guilt – by resurrecting him herself, within herself. When the pressure of his presence became too great she would let him out for a while – she would become him. Her face would screw up in imitation of his face during orgasm. Interspersed with the obscenities and chanteys she would echo the grunts and groans of his passion. When her tension was relieved his character would recede into her, and she would return to her normal life.

When Lindsay and John decided to have a child the pressure was too great to keep hidden any longer. Between the prospect of the tremendous responsibility involved, and her fear that because of some damage her grandfather might have done she would give birth to a monster of some sort, she was unconsciously forced to cry for help. She did this by exposing her alter personality to other people for the first time. Her unconscious plan succeeded – she received the treatment she needed.

Multiple personalities are rare, but when they occur they frequently develop as a reaction to incest guilt. Those therapists who work with multiple personality cases now look for incest in these patients routinely, as more and more reports of incest-induced cases are being made.

Lindsay's grandfather ultimately had to ambush her to achieve his sexual goals. Most grandfather-aggressors, however, resort to subtler methods of seduction. Many of the cases I have seen developed in a fairy tale format, with the grandfather weaving tales of fantasy around sexual activities, anthropomorphizing his penis – giving it human characteristics. Perhaps it is a sleeping prince and only the kiss of a princess will awaken it.

Or it may be an elf who is so lonely that only the kiss of the prettiest little girl in the world will save him from suicide.

One of my patients was molested repeatedly by her grandfather – a minister – who justified his actions by assuring her that it was 'God's will.' In this particular case the girl's mother played a very active silent partner role by sending her daughter to stay with the old man every weekend for three years, despite the fact that he had molested the mother when she was young. The granddaughter eventually went to the authorities and had to testify against her grandfather in court. This was almost as traumatic for her as the actual incest. He was sentenced to prison, piling additional guilt onto her already heavy load.

As in most other forms of incest loneliness plays an important part in motivating grandfather–granddaughter incest, no matter what age the aggressor. In older aggressors, however, that loneliness is, in part, culturally imposed. This form of incest, more than any other, reflects a social problem as much as a private one. It is our neglectful treatment of our aged that precipitates the majority of such cases.

The best prevention of both forms of grandfather–granddaughter incest is for grandparents to lead active lives, getting involved both in their families and in outside interests, where their ability to have normal human relationships will not decay from disuse. A grandfather who is active in the family and with his own friends and interests will not easily sink into the pit of helplessness and loneliness that can lead to incest.

10 · MOTHER–DAUGHTER INCEST

Dear Ann Landers:

I have read several letters in your column about incest, but it's always been a 'Funny Uncle,' a stepdad, a natural father or a brother. Never have you printed a letter about a mother who molested her own daughter. If you've never received one – here's your first.

I am now fifty-eight years old and am speaking of it for the first time. My mother was a teacher and a steady churchgoer. She did the fooling around when she bathed me. I never knew there was anything unusual about her behavior until my father walked in on us and made a terrific scene. (I was twelve years old at that time – much too old to be bathed by my mother.)

She never touched me after that but the damage she had done was considerable. When I married I had a hard time enjoying sex – and still do. I was afraid to bathe my four daughters and had to force myself to do it. Even now I have trouble diapering my granddaughter.

There must be others like me – grown women who still bear the marks of early abuse and have never told a soul. What a relief it has been to write this letter. Bless you.

This is one of the few cases of mother–daughter incest ever published. Since I have only treated a handful of these cases in my practice I searched through a century's worth of psychological, sociological, and sexological books and journals looking for other cases and analyses. Aside from a few briefly sketched cases in two or three popular magazines I was able to find nothing. Even the Greeks, who seemed to have had a godly metaphor for just about every other psychological situation, wrote no tales about mother–daughter incest. Certainly mother–daughter incest is the least understood of all types.

Despite the paucity of research material two traits seem to stand out in the aggressors – they are usually very disturbed women, and they seem to see their daughters as extensions of themselves. These two factors have been apparent in every mother–daughter case I have seen, and I have been told of similar findings by those few of my colleagues who have worked with these aggressors.

The fact that these aggressors are often severely disturbed, possibly psychotic, sets them apart from most other incest aggressors, who generally blend in well with their communities. But were you to see the typical mother–daughter aggressor walking down the street, you might identify her as 'a crazy woman.' More specifically I have found these aggressors to be infantile and extremely needy. They turn to their daughters for emotional feeding, as babies turn to their mothers, effecting a complete role reversal.

Like an infant, the mother who sexually abuses her daughter does not completely differentiate herself from other people. She does not have a sense of herself as an individual, but rather sees her daughter as an extension of herself. She uses the same type of psychological symbolism that is at work in the practice of voodoo, where a doll is substituted for a person in a magic ritual. The daughter becomes the mother's magical symbol for herself. Through this process the aggressor's sexual activity is almost masturbatory. She stimulates her daughter to satisfy her own needs for pleasure.

I am not speaking of strictly sexual needs. As in other forms of incest the sexuality of mother–daughter incest is mostly a response to needs for loving, tenderness, and physical contact. The mother sees her sexual ministrations as demonstrations of affection. These aggressors were often abused or emotionally isolated themselves as children, and may never have learned how to appropriately show affection. Through sexuality with their daughters they seek the loving they have craved all their lives.

The victim senses her mother's neediness, and often puts up with the sexual activity, even if she finds it distasteful, because 'it means so much to mother.' She becomes responsible for satisfying her mother's needs, fulfilling her half of the role reversal by mothering her infantile mother.

At first the victim may enjoy the affectionate caresses, especially if she is too young to understand the sexual nature of her mother's actions – as we shall see in both of the cases in this chapter mother–daughter incest sometimes begins in the daughter's infancy. As the victim grows older, however, the sexuality usually begins to make her feel uncomfortable. She may learn from her friends, from school, or from television that sex is 'naughty.' Or she may feel uneasy about the overt demonstration of her mother's orgasms. Still she will often feel compelled to continue, not because she enjoys the sexual contact, but because she senses her mother's need. In effect she martyrs herself for her mother's pleasure – and she is often consciously aware that she is doing this, as our first case will demonstrate.

Arline Grady

One of my current patients, a victim of mother–daughter incest, is thirty-four-year-old Arline Grady, who came to the hospital recently after a suicide attempt. It was the latest of several. She is in constant emotional chaos; her moods swing radically. She is angry and demanding one minute, then depressed and helpless the next.

Arline is a beautiful woman, about five-and-a-half feet tall, 130 pounds, with blonde hair, a sensual, pretty face, and grey eyes. She has a very seductive manner, especially when she is in the presence of a man.

Arline was born the younger of two sisters, Barbara being three years older than she. Her parents seemed to be compatible; they never fought, but neither did they show each other any public affection. Arline never saw her father give her mother so much as a peck on the cheek.

Her father was a factory worker. Like the rest of his family, he had never graduated from high school, and his wages were low. The family managed to live comfortably, nonetheless, in a small two-bedroom house. Arline shared a room with Barbara.

'My mother was always sick,' Arline recalls. 'She acted crazy. She would talk in what I called "word salads" – her sentences didn't make any sense, her words didn't make any sense. But when my dad came home she stopped and acted normal. I think that's why I think men are so powerful. My dad just turned her off.

'My mother must have weighed 350 pounds. She was very fat, and not very pretty. She was uneducated, but she liked to read.

'I don't know when the sexual stuff began with her because it goes back as far as I can remember. I can picture sitting on her lap and having her touch me, just touching my whole body. She never wore any underwear, and she liked to show me parts of her – her huge breasts, her genitals. And when she bathed me she was very, very thorough. I mean she washed everywhere. She used to stick her finger up my vagina and just keep rubbing, pretending to wash me.

'She was always touching, touching. I couldn't stand it. As early as when I was three I felt uncomfortable with it. Looking back I guess I was starting to break away, to become a little independent. My mother couldn't handle that, and I could sense it. I felt sorry for her. I knew she needed something, that she needed me. I didn't know the touching was abnormal, I was too young, but I knew I didn't want to do it. But she was my mother, so I figured that that's what mothers did.

'She used to play with my sister too. I remember Barbara and my mother would French-kiss, you could see them doing it. My mother always kissed us on the mouth.

'By the time I started school I couldn't stand her to touch me because it made me feel self-conscious. Like if we went downtown or something she always had her arm around me or was touching me somehow. I didn't want her touching me, and because of that I was ashamed of myself. I felt guilty because I knew she needed me.

'My sister was really becoming sexually active at that time, she must have been about eleven. She'd sneak out at night to be with older kids. And she used to masturbate a lot. I remember at night having to listen to her orgasms. I couldn't stand it so I used to sleep on the floor underneath my bed a lot. I remember one day coming home and my sister was having intercourse during the day on the sofa with some guy. My mother was home but she didn't stop it. I think my mother got a vicarious pleasure out of the things my sister did. When Barbara was twelve my parents let her get engaged to this guy who was twenty-six because at least they knew who she was sleeping with at night.

'By that time the sex with my mother had slowed down because I didn't like it. But when she was sad and alone, and my sister was off someplace, I'd go over to her and hold her, and she would start rubbing me. It made her feel better. She used to like me to touch her breasts, but I wouldn't touch her vagina. I think she would have an orgasm; she made the same noises I heard from Barbara at night.

'My sister was beginning to be very violent when I was about eight. She was getting into trouble at school a lot. One night when my parents were out she and three of her girlfriends tried to get me to strip for them and I didn't want to. So Barbara got a knife and they got me on the floor and pinned me down and forced me to lie there while they had oral sex with me. I was terrified. I didn't like women touching me, I never did. After that every time my parents would go to the store or something my sister would bring out her knife and make me strip and lie on the floor and do whatever she wanted. I was scared to death of her. She tried to force me to do things to her, but I wouldn't. So she would have oral sex with me, and push things up my vagina, like sticks and things. I think her relationship with my mother made her very sexually active. She's had several homosexual relationships since she's been an adult. She's also been married four times.

'I don't know why it was, but I always seemed to be getting into situations where I was molested. There was this man in the neighborhood, Uncle Henry – he wasn't really my uncle – and after school he'd have me come over to his house to see his rabbits. He'd take me in back into a shed, and he'd touch me everywhere and have me touch him too.

'Then when I was eleven I went with my family on vacation to Nebraska, where my uncle owned a farm. This was my mother's brother. One night my uncle asked me to walk with him. He gave me a lantern to hold and he put his arm around my waist and his hand went into my pants. I was trying to get his hands, to control them and get him to stop, and then he was pulling me down to the ground and I thought the farmhouse looked really far away – we were in the corn fields – and he had intercourse with me. It was very painful. I kept trying to push him away, but I couldn't. I got hysterical.

'After it was over he held me and I calmed down. My father never touched me, never held me, so I always wanted men to hold me. My mother was so fat and soft and I couldn't stand the feel of a woman's body, but a man – I liked the muscles and the strength and the arms around me. So after my uncle raped me I was always arousing him, trying to get him to hold me, being very seductive.

'Then there was this man who lived around the corner and introduced my sister to sex. I went over there one day and he didn't rape me but he pushed me down on the bed and put his penis in my mouth and made me touch him and offered me a dime and I got sick and all I could think of was getting out of his house.

'After that I fell in love with this boy, but in order for me to go steady with him I had to let all his friends have intercourse with me. His sister was my friend, so I'd spend the night there and five guys would have me in one night. All because I wanted him to love me. I didn't know any better.

'I felt I had to take care of these people because they were weak and I was strong. They needed something, and I could make them feel better. I played the martyr; I didn't know any better. I thought that was what I was there for.

'I didn't realize anything was abnormal with my way of thinking until I was almost twenty, and I had my first child. Then I read all these books about raising children and I realized what I had been doing. I mean I had just been a piece of meat.

'Even after I read all those books I still would go to bed with anybody. It was this martyr thing to some extent, but I also used sex as a weapon. Because my father wouldn't hold me I set out to get every man there was. If there was a woman I particularly disliked, I went after her husband. It's like I set out to seduce the world. I just liked men to say I was pretty and to hold me and say they loved me even if they didn't mean it.

'I didn't know about the passion of sex because I didn't feel anything. I didn't know what the big deal was. I was still frigid when I met my fifth husband when I was twenty-five. I'd just lie back and spread my legs and it wasn't any big deal. I learned how to respond to build their ego so they'd like me, but I didn't feel anything.

'The first time I felt any guilt about sex was when I seduced a priest. I had converted to Catholicism before I married the first time – when I was nineteen – and I was having trouble getting pregnant so I went to confession to confess all these multiple affairs I was having. I mean I was involved with three or four men, plus I was married, plus I was working. I was running this whole office, hiring, training, everything. But messing around with all these guys I was worn out physically.

'Anyway I made my first confession, and the priest said, "No wonder you're tired," and we laughed about it. I went in for counseling and just set out to get him. I mean he didn't seduce me, I seduced him. After that he felt so guilty he had to ask for a transfer. It had never hit me that a man could feel guilty about having sex. After that I went into therapy for the first time.

'My first husband revolted me. I felt like I was being raped every time he came near me. He reminded me of my mother. I couldn't stand for him to touch me. He wasn't attractive, but when I met him he was really, really skinny and homely and he had lost his mother. So I was like his mother. I used to dress him for work and help him brush his teeth and feed him breakfast. I felt sorry for the guy – the martyr again. I had four children with him, and I don't know who fathered any of them except the last one, who was fathered by my second husband while I was still married to my first. My three middle husbands were all losers. I hardly remember them. They treated me like shit.

'Jim, my fifth husband, treated me really well and I wanted to be a perfect wife. I stopped sleeping around and I put all my energy into raising my family right. At that point I started getting terrible migraines. He wasn't mistreating me, he was being really good to me and I couldn't stand the goodness of it all because I couldn't be the martyr anymore. I guess that's why I got the headaches.

'But I really love Jim, and I want this marriage to work. He's the only man who has ever made me climax, but even besides that I really love him.

'I love my children too. I've never had any sexual feelings or fantasies toward them. My oldest son is fourteen and he's a handsome boy, you know, he's developing his muscles, and all I can think of when I look at him is pride. I feel very comfortable touching my children, hugging and kissing them. But I've taught them that adults kiss on the mouth, children kiss on the cheek, and that no one has a right to touch your body unless you want them to.

'I view my children as individuals. My mother never separated me from herself. It's like when she was touching me she was masturbating. It wasn't me that she was doing it to, I was just an extension of her. If my children wiggled when I hugged them I'd immediately let them go because they have a right to determine how much holding they need. And I stopped bathing them as soon as they were old enough to hold a washrag.

'I just don't want my kids to trade off sex for love like I did. I want them to know love, and I think I've taught them that.

'The kind of sexual thing I had with my mother, and that my sister had with my mother, makes it hard to break away as an individual. That's what I've been struggling with in therapy these last few years.

'But now, the way my life is right now ... my outside life is so good. I mean I have four of the most remarkable, sensitive children. It makes me feel good to see my children act so healthy and to have a man who loves me and is supportive. Even though we've had our problems, he's hung in there. I wouldn't change my life.'

Arline's perception of the dynamics of her incest is unusually acute. She speaks of understanding her mother's 'need,' of her own martyrdom, even of feeling she was used as an extension of her mother for masturbatory purposes. Though our therapy sessions have helped her focus on these factors she described already sensing them the first time she told her story in group. From Arline's description it is clear that her mother was a severely disturbed woman. Both Arline and Barbara suffered from their mother's inability to nurture and love them appropriately, and both were easily drawn into the aggressor's sexual activities initially by their own needs for affection.

Though the sisters manifested their reactions to their mother's sexual abuse differently both became extremely self-degrading and hostile. Barbara exhibited her hostility by projecting it from her mother to Arline, sexually abusing her sister in a humiliating, violent manner. Barbara continues to punish herself by substituting sex for love. She moves from one relationship to another, through a series of marriages and homosexual affairs, never finding emotional satisfaction because the only gratification she knows is sexual.

Arline turned her hostility into a sexual vendetta against other women by seducing their husbands. Like her sister Arline used her body indiscriminately to achieve sexual gratification in lieu of emotional fulfillment, despite the fact that she found little physical pleasure in sex. She became reckless with her body, setting herself up to be raped or molested.

When Arline married Jim she found he did not serve her need for punishment. He did not abuse her, he was sensitive enough to arouse her sexually, and he was strong enough not to lean on her. Without punishment Arline could not cope with her guilt and her secret shame. She could not allow herself to live a happy life because she believed that she did not deserve to. So she developed migraines. But even the headaches were not punitive enough to salve her guilt. Eventually she simply lost control and attempted suicide.

It is ironic that after a life of misery Arline has finally found a loving, supportive husband, has raised a healthy family, and only now, when her life seems to be coming together, does she break down. Her treatment is going very slowly.

As is true of all forms of incest the severity of the trauma of mother–daughter incest depends to a great extent on the victim's perception of the nature of the sexual contact. Arline 'couldn't stand' her mother's 'touching,' already feeling uncomfortable about it when she was only three years old. Her mother's 'craziness,' and her sister's violence, created a milieu of psychological disturbance in which the incest trauma expanded freely. This background of disturbance is deeply rooted in Arline's unconscious, making her treatment a plodding, painful process.

But often mother–daughter incest occurs as an exercise – albeit a poor one – in love and tenderness, as in the following case, which, as we shall see, was much less traumatic than Arline's.

Melinda Gilman

I met Melinda Gilman one night at a mutual friend's home. Like a surprising number of people, when she learned that I work extensively with incest patients she volunteered a story of her own. We got together a few days later for an interview. Despite the fact that she had originally offered her story as an incest case, when we met for a lunchtime interview, she insisted that hers was not a case of incest at all. At the outset of the interview she referred to masturbatory experiences with her mother, yet later she claimed that there was nothing sexual about it. Though she claims that she suffered no damage from this relationship she clearly suffers from guilt and doubt, which manifest themselves in her contradictions.

Melinda is a professional poster girl and commercial actress. She has been Miss Coffee, Miss Avocado, Miss Rodeo, and Miss various film festivals. On television she has touted paper towels, coffee, and cooking oil. She is a classic beauty, with silky blonde hair, brown eyes, full lips, and the figure of a starlet. She is thirty years old.

She lives in a small apartment in Hollywood, a few blocks from her mother. They see each other often. Like most incest aggressors Melinda's mother – Betty – was raised in an unloving, abusive environment. Melinda spoke at length about Betty's childhood, believing it explains much of Betty's 'craziness.'

Betty was raised on a farm in Iowa by her father, her stepmother, her sister who was five years older than she, and her stepsister who was her age. Her mother had died during her birth. Melinda described Betty as a Cinderella figure in the midst of three shrewish women. Betty was the only female in the family who could be described as beautiful, and her sister and stepsister constantly made her feel guilty about it – 'Let the princess wash the windows, unless she's too busy looking in the mirror.' Betty's father was often away on business, so she was raised in an atmosphere of animosity.

To escape this Betty went to work as a beautician when she was fifteen. By the time she was seventeen she was managing a shop in Sioux City. At eighteen she married a man who was, in Melinda's words, 'just a punk.' He was young, handsome, loving, and unemployed. In 1943 he went to war. During the next few years Betty worked long and hard, and by the time her husband returned she owned her own beauty shop. Two years later they had Melinda.

When Melinda was born Betty went into a coma. Not knowing what to do with the child Melinda's father left her with her stepgrandmother – the woman who had raised Betty. When Betty finally came out of her coma four months later she seemed to have suffered some sort of minor brain damage, and her relatives tried to take custody of Melinda. Betty had to kidnap her own child, and this set off a feud that divided the family for years.

Melinda was all Betty had left in the world. During her illness her beauty shop had closed down. Her husband had disappeared with her savings. And her family had turned against her.

The process of rebuilding her life was difficult, but Betty did it for Melinda. By the time her husband had run through her money and returned three years later she owned a shop and was saving for a second.

The day he came back Melinda was sitting in a rocker outside the beauty shop. She saw a man circling the block several times. Finally he stopped the car and called her name. As she recalls, 'I got freaked and I went running in to my mother, crying. I said, "Some man out there scared me." She ran out, took a look, pulled in the rocker, locked the door, pulled the shade down, and said, "It's all right, honey. There's no one there."'

But there was. He called repeatedly until Betty agreed to see him. Then he charmed her into taking him back. Melinda was almost four.

'I hated him,' says Melinda. 'He was foreboding. The only thing he knew how to instill in me was fear. When he finally left again when I was six you don't know how happy I was.'

It was about this time that Melinda became aware of her mother's 'touching.'

'It probably started when I was born,' she says. 'You see, my mother's a very "touchy" person, she's very sensual. We used to have masturbatory experiences together. She would like sensitize me. When I was growing up I got my first sexual turn-on from her. Maybe my first orgasm. She would tickle me and we would cuddle.

'It became a ritual, every night. I would go to bed and my mother would come in and sit by me and just start tickling and massaging me. Then she would say, "Now you tickle me," and I would, but never the genitals. That made me feel strange. I would just kind of skirt around them, like a game.

'I felt that my mother got a lot of enjoyment out of it. She must have been really unfulfilled sexually. I mean my father was always running off. Once when I was about six she had an affair with a woman who worked with her, and who moved in to live with us. My mother was a very loose kind of woman, very different from me. She knew no boundaries.

'We used to bathe together until I was about seven, but then I became very modest, I mean prudishly so. I guess it was because my mother was so open about sex. She used to talk about it very openly, and I didn't like that. She always found it amusing that I was so sensitive about sex.

'With me it was always just love. There was nothing incestuous about it. It was sensuality without sexuality. That's why I don't consider the touching with my mother to be a sexual thing. Because I didn't feel uncomfortable about it – at least not until I was about thirteen. It was just love. My mother just loved me. She would say, "You're real pretty; you're my baby; I love you," and she would just caress me. It was very nice. It was really great.

'But we were very different, and after I reached my teens we didn't get along too well. She would start to do it and I would say, "Mother, stop it!" I started thinking about these things, and I didn't like the idea that my mother was doing this to me. It was like I felt the same kind of warmth that

I felt for a boyfriend or something. I mean it felt good, but when you start to know about your body you start putting up barriers.

'I don't believe in barriers anymore. It's not that I'm not moral, but I've grown a lot. I think now it would be great to have sex with my mother. I mean I personally have fantasies about women that age. I imagine myself their confidant, pretending that I am their daughter, and in my fantasy I would find them very sensual. I slept with an older woman once, but she was only a few years older than me. I liked it because she was a very special person to me. You can't separate emotion from sex.

'That's why I say that I would like to sleep with my mother, because the emotions are still there. I love her in a deep, deep, deep, overwhelming way – yet I don't get along with her. I find her offensive; she's very judgmental. She really infuriates me most of the time. And she has really terrible taste – she bleaches her hair platinum, and she wears ridiculously too much makeup. She's very tacky. She makes me feel very uptight and uncomfortable.

'She's always been a little bit crazy. She could walk off with something from someone's house or from a store, or she could say something embarrassing, like a racist remark or something. She's very unpredictable. I don't think she has any morals. I had to find my own.'

Melinda has been living a reclusive life lately. Her relationships with men never seem to work out for her. 'There are nothing but jerks in this town,' she says of the men she has encountered. 'So I've just been keeping to myself. Who needs the aggravation? I spend nice quiet evenings alone and get to sleep by ten o'clock. It's lovely.'

Melinda describes her mother as being 'a little bit crazy,' fitting our model of the disturbed mother–daughter aggressor. It is apparent from Melinda's account that her mother was an emotionally needy woman – apparently trying to compensate for her abusive upbringing by demanding affection from her daughter. Melinda felt that her mother needed her very much, and perceived the sexual contact as a fulfillment of that need. Betty would initiate the classic role reversal by asking Melinda to 'tickle' her. In responding to her mother's request for physical nurturing Melinda would act as mother – Betty's symbolic extension of herself.

This role reversal was confusing to Melinda, and, coupled with her guilt over having participated in and having enjoyed the incest, causes her to resent her mother, to become hostile. When Betty and Melinda are together they invariably argue. Melinda's love for her mother is pitted against her anger. This ambivalence is even more apparent in her intonation than it is in her words. She loves, she hates; she admires, she is ashamed; she is attracted, she is repelled. Classic conflicts of incest.

Her inability to relate well to her mother is mirrored in her inability to develop stable relationships with men. Typically she has trouble communicating with and trusting men. So she has withdrawn from social contacts entirely. Instead of seeking help she has pulled into a shell. She calls her reclusiveness 'lovely,' but she means 'nonthreatening.'

Her relations with men are further complicated by the fact that she was 'sensitized' by her mother, learning to associate sexuality with her mother's caresses. Her fantasies deal not with men, but with older women – mother figures. She vicariously acts out her compulsion to repeat her incestuous experience by becoming sexually attracted to older women. This is her way of reconciling her incestuous desires with the incest taboo.

The physical relations between mother and daughter in the two cases we have looked at were similar in many respects. Both daughters felt that they were making their mothers feel good; they both admitted that they enjoyed the caresses at first, before they became aware of the taboo they were violating; and they both grew to dislike the contact. Despite the differences between these mothers and other incest aggressors the incest conflicts experienced by the victims are strikingly similar. These conflicts arise primarily from guilt.

With few cases to draw conclusions from, and no significant material in the literature, it is difficult to make any sweeping generalizations about mother–daughter victims, though the nature of the aggressors seems more clearcut. My mother–daughter patients respond slowly to treatment; the incest wound is particularly deep in these victims. Their incest trauma is compounded by the fact that a mother capable of incest with her daughter is generally incapable of providing the normal mothering that is so vital to a child's development. The first link in the chain of psychological development – the mother–child love bond – is substantially contorted. Even with treatment it can only be partially restored.

11 · FATHER–SON INCEST

Father–son incest is considered especially repulsive in our society because it violates so many taboos and cultural standards. Not only is there incest, but there is homosexual activity, introducing a child to homosexuality, and often sodomy (anal intercourse) – usually in the form of rape. The father–son victim can be terribly affected, not only because of the incest betrayal, the culturally imposed guilt of homosexual contact, and the pain of anal penetration if there is any, but because he usually grows to hate his father. And if he hates his father – his role model – he hates a large part of himself. The feelings of guilt common to all incest victims are compounded in father–son cases by this particularly painful form of self-loathing.

Father–son incest seems to stem more from a psychological breakdown in the father than from a family breakdown. Instead of reflecting the aggressor's present conflicts, father–son incest is often motivated by problems in the aggressor's youth – homosexual conflicts, a domineering mother, feelings of inadequacy, and so on. In this personal breakdown we see some parallels between father–son and mother–daughter aggressors. In both patterns of incest the problem seems to be less a family one than a personal one. But father–son aggressors don't seem to be as overtly disturbed as do mother–daughter aggressors. Incestuous fathers are more successful at keeping their conflicts hidden.

HOMOSEXUAL CONFLICTS

Many father–son aggressors are motivated by homosexual conflicts from their youth. For example, in 1968 psychiatrist Donald G. Langsley and two colleagues, from the University of Colorado School of Medicine, reported a case of father–son incest in which the father had had enjoyable homosexual relations as a boy with his cousin, and later with a friend. He named his son after the friend. Father and son began weight-training together when the boy was twelve, and after each session they would massage each other's muscles and genitals. This continued for one-and-a-half years. During this time the father tried to set his son up with a cousin – the son of the father's first homosexual lover. The father–son victim became increasingly disturbed in his mid-teens, eventually drifting into heavy drug use. During an episode of uncontrollable LSD hallucinations he was taken to a hospital, and there he revealed the incest to the attending physician.

Langsley and his colleagues investigated the case and found that during the period of the father–son incest there was no particular upheaval in the family, no special conflicts, no change in the father's sexual relations with his wife, and certainly no abnormalities that would make the family seem out of the ordinary to other community members. The researchers concluded that the father was clearly acting out his own adolescent homosexual conflicts: 'That he repeats with his own son some of his own earlier sexual conflicts is striking, even to putting his son in bed with the son of the cousin with whom he had had his first homosexual satisfaction.'

INADEQUACY AND THE DOMINEERING MOTHER

Generally, however, homosexuality seems to be a secondary motivation in father–son cases. Father–son aggressors more often use incest in an attempt to cope with feelings of inadequacy. Such feelings are often due to an overbearing, powerful mother. Such a mother controls her son's life so strictly that he never develops confidence in being able to accomplish anything on his own. Later in life he turns to incest as an exercise in power, an attempt to control something on his own – something of which his mother would doubtless disapprove.

These motives are clear in the first case we will examine. Homosexual motives seem only peripheral – in fact the aggressor committed incest with his daughter also.

Ben Taber

Ben Taber first entered one of my outpatient groups because he had great difficulty relating to others. His best – and only – friend had committed suicide. His wife had left him. He was afraid to talk to people, afraid they wouldn't like him. When I first saw him I was struck by how bland and withdrawn he was, as if his personality were forced to leak out drop by drop because he was afraid to open the tap. He spoke in a barely audible monotone.

I learned very little about Ben in treatment, for he refused to open up. He remained in my group for only two sessions, then he dropped out. He did, however, subsequently allow me to interview him at length, and he arranged for me to interview his sister, Jill. Between the two of them I was able to put together not only their story, but an outline of their father's youth.

Their father, Andrew Taber, was born and raised in Newark, New Jersey. When he was an infant his father deserted the family, but his mother, who had always supported the family anyway, was able to maintain their upper-class lifestyle. She and her sister were partners in a business they had founded, and together they amassed a considerable fortune.

Andrew's childhood was tightly controlled. His mother ruled with an iron foot, and she seemed to put it down every time he attempted to assert himself, every time he reached for a bit of independence.

After graduating from high school at sixteen Andrew went into his mother's business, where he learned the basic rudiments of accounting. There she could be not only mother, but boss. But when his mother took him into the business she had not counted on his falling in love with an eighteen-year-old secretary. The young couple married two weeks after they met. Andrew's mother spent the next three years trying to get the marriage annulled. After all, he was only sixteen – still her baby!

Despite the hatred that developed between Andrew's mother and his wife the newlyweds lived with the matriarch for their first few years of marriage. Finally Andrew's wife became pregnant, and his mother gave up the battle against the marriage and had a pleasant little three-bedroom stucco house built for them on a nearby lot. Behind the house was a large oak tree in which Andrew built a tree house for his forthcoming child.

Then Ben was born. Andrew was at work when he heard the news, and the first thing he did was rush to his mother's house. Together they went to the hospital.

Andrew had hoped that Ben's birth would change his life. He had hoped that his relationship with his wife would grow closer, and that he would feel more like a man. But his mother continued to control their lives through her control of the purse strings, and his wife continually badgered him about it. She wanted him to get another job, to leave his mother's business. But he had no marketable skills, no college degree, and no confidence in himself. When he looked in the mirror he saw a scrawny, sickly man with no future – his mother had been telling him since he was a child that he would die before he was twenty-one; he had suffered grand mal epileptic seizures since infancy.

A year-and-a-half later his daughter Jill was born. By then he had begun to vent his frustrations on his wife by occasionally beating her. In violence he discovered power.

Andrew's new-found power at home was beginning to manifest itself in his relationship with his mother. He began to challenge her authority. She, in turn, enlisted psychiatrists to strengthen her hold. Once, for example, Andrew decided he would take his family to the country for a brief vacation. His mother disapproved, and had a psychiatrist on her payroll declare Andrew unsound. The psychiatrist arrived at Andrew's house with two attendants, who placed Andrew in a straitjacket. When his wife tried to intervene one of the attendants knocked her to the floor, and the psychiatrist told her that she was to blame for Andrew's 'mental illness.' The children looked on in disbelief.

Andrew began beating his children as soon as they were old enough to get into trouble. He kept a variety of sticks handy for a variety of offenses, and when the offense was sufficiently severe he would bring out the belt. As he beat his children – invariably in front of each other – he would smile.

His wife had become a bitter woman. She would often call Jill an unwanted child – 'an accident' – and she would often remind her husband that she had married him not for love but for money. 'If I had known that it was all *hers*,' she would say, referring to her mother-in-law, 'I never would have married you.'

When Jill was six Andrew began molesting her when his wife was not at home. He started by bouncing her on his knee as most fathers do with their daughters, then he began reaching into her panties as he bounced her. At first she enjoyed the sensation of his rubbing, but her strict Catholic upbringing made her feel guilty. Visions of Hell came to her mind. She asked him to stop. He did, for the time being.

As time went on Andrew became more forceful in his sexual advances toward Jill, and she, torn between this new feeling of intimacy and her guilt, reluctantly gave in. The incest resumed when she was eight.

'In my father's own way,' she says, 'I at least knew he loved me. It was clear from day one that mother didn't. I remember I would get undressed to take a bath, and he would come in and start playing. He wouldn't be affectionate like hugging or kissing, but he would tell me how pretty I was – and I knew he wasn't talking about my face, but about my vagina. I would try to deal with it by laughing it off. But I was scared, and I didn't know what I was scared of. It kept getting worse. He would ask me to touch his genitals, then he would try to force me to perform fellatio on him, literally pushing my head down on him. I would beg him to stop, and we would physically fight about it, but at this point he was much stronger than I was, so he had his way. He hadn't started in on Ben yet, so I was taking the brunt of his aggressiveness.

'When he would fondle me he never masturbated himself. I don't think he had to. I think he got off on the power trip.'

Andrew first turned sexually to his son when Ben was about twelve. 'He was in the living room reading a pornographic magazine,' Ben recalls. 'I came in and sat down beside him and he made some reference to some of the pictures. He could see that I was getting turned on. At that time the only sexual contact I had had was a homosexual relationship with a friend of mine. We had had oral sex a few times. Nothing serious, just messing around. I had enjoyed it, but I felt guilty. My friend led me into it. He had had a relationship with his grandfather. Eventually the guilt got to me, so I stopped hanging around with him.

'My father asked me if I had ever had sex with anybody, so I told him about this relationship and we began fondling each other's sex organs. It really turned me on. My mother was home, so we went out to the tree house and had oral sex. It was something I wanted as much as he did. I liked it. It felt good. I didn't have a very close relationship with my father before this.

'When I was fourteen I started getting very rebellious. I wouldn't do anything that my parents told me to do. At the time I was also having a relationship with my sister. We would go over to my grandmother's place, and she had this roomer who had some nudist magazines. So we would look at the magazines, then have oral sex. That's when I found out that my sister was having a relationship with my father. That made me jealous – of him, not her. I wanted my sister's affection, so I was having a lot of trouble getting along with him. He used to have to call the police on me a lot. There were several times when it got violent.

'The sexual thing with my father went on until I was sixteen and started dating. As a teenager I was always trying to prove my manhood. I was drinking a lot. I was in a very rough crowd, and I did a lot of things with the guys – burglarizing places and stuff like that. By that time I was strictly heterosexual, though I preferred oral sex to intercourse. It wasn't until years later that I realized I could get a girl to climax by intercourse.'

When Ben was nineteen the relationship with his father almost came to light. He had been having a particularly violent fight with his father, and Andrew had called the police. When they arrived Jill reacted to what she saw as the injustice of Ben's being taken away for something that was Andrew's fault. In desperation she cried, 'You don't understand what goes on here! My father's a pervert! He tried to rape me! My brother isn't the bad person, it's my father! He does all kinds of perverted things to me!'

Jill recalls that the police seemed to pretend nothing had been said. They gave Ben a warning and left quickly. 'My mother's eyeballs almost fell out onto the floor,' she says. 'She was in shock. Then she started ranting about how I was just making it up because I hated my father so much. She wouldn't believe it.'

That incident pretty much marked the end of the sexual contact between Andrew and either of his children. By that time both Ben and Jill were physically stronger than Andrew, whose health was deteriorating just as his mother had said it would, so they had little trouble rebuffing his advances. His attempts at sexual contact had become pathetic; his children had grown strong enough to control *him*. He encountered in them the domination from which he had first tried to escape by tyrannizing his family. His problem had come full circle. His failing health forced him to take drugs that slowly destroyed his sense of balance. At forty-two he took a gun and shot himself in the head.

From his incest experience, coupled with the generally miserable quality of his home life, Ben developed serious personality problems – extreme shyness, insecurity, inability to communicate with others, and discomfort with his sexual identity. We have discussed most of these symptoms before in the context of other forms of incest, but the problem with sexual identity is especially prevalent in father–son cases. Because of his ambivalent feelings about his father – his role model – Ben is unable to feel comfortable in either a heterosexual or a homosexual role. His first sexual pleasure was derived from another penis, directing him toward men as sexual objects; yet that pleasure was wrapped in painful guilt, repelling him from men. Women, on the other hand, intimidate him because he associates them with his cold, unloving mother, his domineering, castrating grandmother, and his sister, who rejected him by cutting off their sexual relationship. He remains in sexual purgatory.

Andrew used sex as an exercise in power. Whether he was having relations with Ben, Jill, or his wife his motivations were identical – to attain dominance (it wasn't until both Ben and Jill were physically able to repel his sexual advances that he finally stopped). He was not after sexual gratification, he was after independence from his mother – power of his own.

Andrew's wife played the part of the classic silent partner. She was a cold, unloving woman, and rejected both her husband and her children. Not only did her emotional neglect of the family contribute to the incest motives of all three active participants, but when the incest was exposed she denied it, accusing Jill of lying. Though it is possible that Andrew's need to escape his mother's dominance might have caused him to abuse his children no matter what role his wife played, her neglect certainly increased the odds.

As tragic as this case may seem it is the lesser of two father–son incest evils. There was at least a semblance of tenderness in Ben's relationship with his father, some degree of mutual pleasure. In many cases, however, the father forcibly sodomizes his son. These victims tend to be much more severely disturbed by the experience as the following case illustrates.

Michael Blake

Last year fourteen-year-old Michael Blake was transferred to the hospital from a county placement in a boys' ranch. He was an unusually handsome boy – thick, straight black hair, deep blue eyes, high cheekbones, a well-developed body.

Michael had been in foster homes since his mother ran away when he was two years old. Recently he had been transferred to the boys' ranch. For a few months he seemed to blend in well enough with the other boys, but after a Christmas visit with his father he began to withdraw, to disregard authority, and to talk of suicide. He was caught stealing in school, and he began fighting with the other boys. He was totally uncooperative whenever teachers or counselors tried to find out what was wrong. Finally he attempted suicide by swallowing a handful of cold tablets, and he was sent to the psychiatric hospital.

Michael was difficult from the beginning. He resented being in the hospital, repeatedly asserting that he was not 'crazy.' On his admissions form there was a short questionnaire entitled 'Personal Data.' This is how he filled it in:

Q. How well do you get along with other people?

A. It depends.

Q. What thing, persons, situation, or activities make you upset, tense, anxious, or blue?

A. Thinking of my past life.

Q. What are you likely to do when upset, uncomfortable, tense, anxious, or blue?

A. Run, try to hurt myself, or break something.

Q. What would a person who knows you well say if he were asked to describe your good points?

A. I have no idea.

Q. What would a person who knows you well say if he were asked to describe your bad points?

A. I'm not very honest. I can't trust anyone.

We hoped that one of my adolescent groups, where his peers might give him some positive feedback, would build up his self-esteem.

At first he was silent, refusing to participate in any discussions, and refusing to respond to questions with anything more than grunts. Then one day I brought in some batakas – foam rubber bats used for pounding out aggressions.

'Why don't you try one?' I asked. 'Go on. Beat the hell out of that chair. It'll make you feel good.'

'Oh, no,' he replied. 'If I got started I'd never stop. There's just too much anger inside me. I'd probably lose control. Then I'd really be crazy.'

'Go on, give it a try.'

'No. I'm not ready.' But he picked up a bataka tentatively, just toying with it. He looked it over for several minutes, until the silence in the room became oppressive. The other kids seemed to sense his tension, and they waited patiently, hoping he would let his feelings out as most of them had done at one time or another.

'Come on, Michael,' I finally said. 'Either do it or get off the pot. I'm going to count to three. If you don't get down to working on this by then we'll move on to someone else.'

On the count of two he hit the chair with a loud thwack. He paused for a moment, then hit it again. Then slowly, like a train pulling out of a station, he began to accelerate his pace until his arm was a blur. Again and again he smashed the chair, and slowly a scream built in his throat until he was pouring out sound and sweat and pain.

'I hate you! I hate you! How could you! I hate you! You filthy, dirty bastard! I trusted you! How could you! You were all I had! All I had . . .' And finally he collapsed on the floor in tears. Several group members converged on him, hugging him, reassuring him. After he had calmed down he haltingly told his story.

He had gone to see his father for Christmas vacation. On Christmas day his father began drinking early. By late afternoon he was drunk, and he told Michael that he wanted to 'fool around a little.' When Michael refused his father pulled out a straight razor.

'You're a real pretty boy,' he said. 'A real pretty boy. Your face has grown real handsome since the last time I saw you. Real pretty. You wouldn't want me to cut it up for you, would you pretty boy?'

His father wrestled Michael to the ground, cutting him lightly on the face and hands in the process. Then, with the razor held tightly against Michael's cheek, his father sodomized him. It was an ugly, painful rape, with no pretense of tenderness or affection.

After Michael finished his story a pretty blonde girl named Melissa said to him, 'And I thought I had problems.' That brought a broad grin to his face, the first any of us had seen. He and Melissa were inseparable thereafter, and both of them seemed to be improving quickly.

Unfortunately Michael's state medical insurance ran out soon after, and he had to leave the hospital. He was transferred to the adolescent unit of a county hospital for long-term psychiatric treatment. The day he left he came to see me in the nurses' station where I was doing some paperwork. 'Will you marry me?' he asked. 'No,' I said gently. 'Well then, will you adopt me?' 'No . . .' He threw his arms around me and we held each other tightly. Both of us were in tears. It was one of the most painful goodbyes I've ever had to say.

At the county hospital, isolated from Melissa and from the first caring environment he had ever known, he lapsed into a deep depression. As we go to press he seems to be improving, but his condition is very delicate. In a letter he wrote to me recently he said, 'I'm trying real hard to get my head together. I think I'm doing better . . . at least I don't think about dying so much.'

In his discharge record from the first hospital it is interesting to note that mention was made of 'homosexual rape,' but not of the fact that it was by his father. Such omissions are common, yet often, as in this case, potentially damaging to treatment. Incest was the central trauma in Michael's case, and to ignore it in treatment would do him a grave disservice. He may repress it and never mention it again, in which case succeeding therapists would have no focus for their treatment. In assuming that homosexual rape was the basis of Michael's trauma the attending physician overlooked the incest trauma entirely. Such an oversight can be disastrous – incest is never irrelevant.

The two cases in this chapter have certain elements in common, elements I have also observed over the years in the other father–son cases I have seen. There is often a breakdown in the family, but in father–son incest this breakdown often includes the father's trying to reach out for satisfaction of needs that are beyond the scope of even a well-adjusted family.

Ben's father was trying to find strength and self-confidence, trying to break away from his own mother by exercising power. Michael's father's motives remain a mystery, since he left town hurriedly after the incest incident, and has yet to be heard from. But the brutality of the rape suggests the father's hostility, anger, and frustration, and perhaps some jealousy at Michael's youth and good looks. Michael's extreme reaction to his incestuous experience reflects not only the violence of the rape, but the indignity of the sodomy. A man in our society is raised to require confidence and self-respect, to feel dominant, and when these feelings are negated by his own father, he loses not only his dignity, but his identity. Both Ben and Michael considered themselves less than human, so they acted as if they were less than human.

You could say that both Ben and Michael were victims of psychological murder. That is the best metaphor I can use to describe the intensity of emotional violence father–son victims – and for that matter, most other incest victims – undergo. And because father–son victims are rarely willing or able to testify against their fathers, murder is what these aggressors usually get away with.

12 · INCEST AND THE LAW

Incest carries criminal penalties in every state. Yet there is something about incest that seems to elevate it above the common statutes of man: to most people incest seems to be a violation of 'God's laws.' The impulse of most juries is to throw the book at the 'monster' who commits incest. In *Crime in Modern Society* M. Elliot pointed out that of eighty-nine cases of incest tried in Wisconsin in the early 1950s, more than half of the aggressors were convicted of rape rather than incest because rape carried a longer sentence.

Yet a punitive attitude toward incest serves neither the aggressor, the victim, nor the community. Legal action should be aimed, whenever possible, at reuniting the family by directing both victim and aggressor to enter treatment, and by suggesting that the silent partner join them. Since numerous studies have suggested that convicted incest offenders have one of the lowest rates of recidivism of all categories of crime it is rarely productive to tear the family apart by sentencing the aggressor to prison. Society is best served by minimizing the victim's guilt – such as guilt over being responsible for sending a parent to prison – so that he or she is less likely to drift into antisocial behavior; by eliminating the expense of unnecessary incarceration; and by eliminating the expense of supporting the aggressor's family through welfare. The imposition of appropriate sentencing must be dictated by society's needs, not its rage.

Most American incest statutes date back to the nineteenth century. Since then most states have reduced incest penalties from as much as life imprisonment to the present range of from one to fifteen years.

Legal definitions of incest vary from state to state. Parents and children, brothers and sisters are always 'within the degrees of consanguinity within which marriages are declared to be incestuous and void.' Aunts and nephews, uncles and nieces are usually included. Beyond that there is a wide range. In Alabama incest includes parents and stepchildren, and fathers-in-law and daughters-in-law. In Mississippi half children are included, but stepchildren are not. Texas includes adopted children in its definition. Utah will prosecute sexual partners as far as fourth cousins, and prohibits marriage between fifth cousins. Oregon considers only direct ancestors and descendants, and half- or full siblings in its definition of incest.

Aside from laws against incest many states have laws mandating that incest be reported by any medical, social service, school or law enforcement official who suspects it. The California reporting law (PC# 11161.5) is typical of the bills being passed. It requires any

physician and surgeon, dentist, resident, intern, podiatrist, chiropractor, religious practitioner, registered nurse, school superintendent, supervisor of child welfare and attendance, certified pupil personnel employee, school principal, teacher, licensed day care worker ... administrator of a public or private summer day camp or child care center or social worker [to report any suspected abuse by telephone *and* in writing within thirty-six hours to] both the local police authority having jurisdiction and to the juvenile probation department; or, in the alternative, either to the county welfare department, or to the county health department.

To protect these mandated professionals from being sued for slander or libel the law indemnifies anyone who reports suspected abuse against all civil or criminal liability.

An important California Supreme Court ruling in 1976 made anyone mandated to report abuse who neglected to do so liable for any subsequent damages incurred by the child. The precedent was set by the case of eleven-month-old Gita Landeros, who was taken to the doctor to have a broken leg set. The nature of the break, other bruises, and her fear of people were typical of what doctors have come to identify as 'the battered child syndrome' (the reporting of both suspected battered children and sexually abused children is mandated by the same law). The doctor ignored these symptoms, however, simply setting the leg and sending Gita back into the abusive home.

She appeared at another hospital two months later with a black eye, puncture wounds on her back and leg, bite marks on her face, and a left hand that was so badly scalded that she lost the use of it. This time the abuse was reported, and the subsequent investigation revealed the original doctor's oversight. Gita's court-appointed guardian sued the doctor in her behalf for the injuries she had suffered because the doctor had not intervened when he should have. Aside from the doctor's criminal liability – a misdemeanor – the court held that he was *civilly* liable. This meant that he could be made to pay substantial damages.

Thus the penalties for noncompliance with the law became substantial. Hospitals, which had previously been lax in informing their personnel about reporting law requirements, began circulating memos and forms, for they too could be named in suits.

Reporting violations cause significant problems for psychiatrists who are torn between reporting and respecting doctor–patient confidentiality. What does the psychiatrist do when a patient comes to him and says, 'Doctor, I need help with a problem, but you've got to promise not to go to the police. I'll enter any program you prescribe; I'll do anything; but I don't want the authorities brought in. I've been sleeping with my daughter.'? Under the law the psychiatrist must report the man. But this discourages many aggressors from seeking help. The choice is a difficult one to make, and professionals are split on how to react to such situations.

Yet there is a significant advantage to reporting an aggressor: The court system creates a powerful wedge to force reticent aggressors into treatment. Even when aggressors go into therapy voluntarily they often back out when the sessions become emotionally threatening. Given the choice of treatment or jail the aggressor is much more likely to endure the pain of treatment.*

Unfortunately reporting an aggressor does not guarantee that he will be brought to trial, nor that the court will place him in a treatment program if he is convicted. There is a complex tangle of legal and psychological factors that often impedes effective justice and treatment. The situation is similar in many respects to the judicial problems that rape cases presented a few years ago, before public outcry forced at least some changes in the system – the victim is often accused of lying or having 'asked for it,' she may be humiliated by the defense attorney if she goes to court, she may be afraid to accuse her abuser, she may be embarrassed to make a public admission, etc.

* In the United Kingdom there is no obligation of this kind to report incest, although a Chief Officer of Police must report any offense of incest alleged to have been committed within his Police District to the Director of Public Prosecutions.

Because father–daughter cases account for 75 percent of the incest cases that wind up in court I will focus on this type of incest to illustrate the legal process. However the discussion in this chapter applies to all forms of incest.

OBSTACLES TO JUSTICE

When an incest case is brought to light the victim's first problem is to decide whether to press charges against the aggressor. Like the rape victim the incest victim is understandably reticent to recount the graphic details of her incestuous relationship before a courtroom of strangers. As the case we will examine in this chapter reveals, the incest victim is often badgered and degraded by the defense attorney as he attempts to discredit her story.

Aside from the anguish of the courtroom the victim must struggle with her love for her father. As we have seen throughout this book the incestuous contact is often the only 'loving' the child has ever known, and she may still feel close to her father. This makes it difficult for her to testify against him, and perhaps be responsible for sending him to prison. She has enough guilt to deal with without having to feel responsible for the imprisonment of her father and the possible impoverishment of the rest of her family. The victim also might be pressured by her mother to drop the allegations.

If the victim *does* decide to prosecute, she may run into a series of judicial obstacles. In some cases she may find the matter handled quietly in juvenile court, which frequently involves her temporary placement in a juvenile hall until the case is adjudicated. Such placement can be very damaging to a young victim, for she experiences being removed from her home as punishment for the incest – which, in turn, reinforces her feelings of responsibility for the incest.

In many states – New York, for example – a child's testimony alone is not enough to sustain a guilty verdict against an aggressor, and since there is often no corroborating witness to incest, charges are often dropped or reduced. In other states prosecutors often feel – justifiably or not – that the testimony of a young child will not be acceptable in court, so they do not prosecute cases involving preteen victims. But according to Superior Court Judge Peter Giannini, who presides over juvenile proceedings in Los Angeles County, 'The fact that the child may be five doesn't mean she doesn't have the capacity to testify. I take the child into my chambers and talk with her. All she needs to know to be a qualified witness is the difference between right and wrong.' This qualification is the standard in the state of California, and similar standards hold in most states.*

The experience of pressing charges and testifying in an incest trial can be almost as traumatic to a victim as the incest act itself. The pressures of reliving the experience, of public humiliation, of testifying against a parent, and of potential financial hardship are tremendous. The incest victim is usually in a precarious psychological state to begin with, and these pressures can push her over the edge.

SENTENCING THE AGGRESSOR

Once the psychological and legal obstacles are overcome, and the aggressor is found guilty, the major weakness of the system is revealed – the court's hands are usually tied by the unavailability of appropriate incest treatment programs, so the aggressor must either go to prison or be allowed to go free and untreated on probation. Most judges who deal with incest cases recognize that most aggressors need treatment more than imprisonment.

Incest aggressors very rarely repeat their crime, once caught. An American research project on recidivism conducted by B. C. Glueck, Jr., between 1952 and 1955, showed that of 1,146 American sex offenders, incest offenders were by far the most infrequent repeaters. A Danish study of criminals convicted of sexual offenses between 1929 and 1939 revealed that only 2 percent of the incest offenders returned to prison for incest, yet the overall recidivism rate was almost 25 percent for other crimes, and for sexual offenses specifically, 10 percent. Psychologist Hank Giarretto, director of the world's largest and most successful organized incest program, in Santa Clara, California, reports that fewer than 1 percent of his more than three thousand patients have attempted to repeat their incestuous offenses.

Most incest aggressors are not dangerous criminals, and do not need to be locked up. The purpose of our penal system is supposed to be rehabilitation, and the incest aggressor can best be rehabilitated in

* In the United Kingdom if the victim had consented then she or he would be an accomplice and their evidence would have to be corroborated.

treatment. Unfortunately there are less than a handful of qualified treatment programs in the United States today, so most courts have no alternative to prison.

Alison Mulray

I had learned about the various problems of the legal system's approach to incest from patients' descriptions throughout the years, but I had my first opportunity to see the system at work when I attended an incest trial last year while researching this book.

The defendant's name was Don Mulray, and he was accused by his youngest daughter – fifteen-year-old Alison – of repeated oral sex and intercourse. After the trial Alison's mother, Karen, agreed to an interview, and a few days later I spoke briefly to Alison herself. From the trial transcript and these two interviews I pieced together the family story.

Karen Mulray is an intelligent, attractive woman in her mid-forties. She lives with her second husband, William, in a beautiful middle-class suburban home with clipped hedges, a white oak on the front lawn, and a brick driveway. She still maintains the trim figure she had twenty years ago when she met her first husband, Don.

A description of Don would be incomplete if I didn't note his uncanny resemblance to the classic figure of Mephistopheles. He wears a goatee – half-black, half-gray. His hair recedes into a bald spot, and his eyes are gray, colorless. He is a tall, lanky man.

Karen first met Don in college; they were both studying to be teachers. She found him attractive, intelligent, and aggressive. 'Sexually he was a very odd combination,' she recalls. 'He wanted sex very, very badly. That was one of the things that bothered me before we were married. He wanted to have sex, and I wanted to wait until we were married. But rather than pay any attention to my feelings, he practically forced himself on me one night, which really scared me. That should have been a good indication of trouble, but he made all these intellectualizations about how we were going to be married anyway so what difference did it make. I shouldn't have believed him, but I was exceptionally dumb for twenty-one. Even eleven-year-olds aren't as naïve today as I was then. Anyway it was just sort of spur of the moment thing while we were sitting in the car in front of the house. He was very definitely trying to penetrate me, but he lost his erection and couldn't do anything.

'After we got married we had sex three times a day for several months, if not years. Gradually he worked it down to once a day, which still seemed like a tremendous burden to me. There was no satisfaction at all in it for me. He would maintain an erection for maybe thirty seconds after penetration, then he would ejaculate and it would be over. After about five years we finally worked out a routine with manual efforts that satisfied me. By that time we had the two girls, Kelly and Alison.

'We had other things going for us, though. We enjoyed the outdoors and camping, and we got into collecting bottles. The bottles took over our lives, and they eventually destroyed the marriage. He was always complaining about not having enough money, and nagging about it. But then he became obsessed with bottles, and got to the point where he spent three hundred dollars on a bottle without even telling me.

'Then he brought this bottle collector home. He was a bachelor and a really good friend of Don's. This fellow started making a play for me behind Don's back. He wasn't handsome, but he really turned me on. Somehow he understood how much was missing from my relationship with Don, how much I needed that flirting, how a man is supposed to treat a woman – all that stuff Don never did. I never realized how much I was missing until this guy started in, just talking – but in a seductive way. My brains told me I didn't want to get involved with this guy, but "down there" I was really turned on. Because of all this I knew something was wrong, so I went to a therapist. Eventually that finished the marriage: I realized I couldn't go on the way we were. Don refused to go into therapy with me, so we got a divorce in 1968, after eleven years of marriage. The girls were nine and eleven.'

Three years after the divorce Karen remarried. She and her new husband, William, had custody of the girls. Kelly pretty much cut herself off from her natural father. Although she saw him regularly she kept her distance. Alison, however, seemed quite close to Don.

When Kelly was sixteen she became interested in music, and spent a great deal of time composing and practicing the guitar. Her mother had no idea that Kelly had lost interest in boys, becoming attracted, instead, to other girls. Alison's behavior, on the other hand, was blatantly trouble-some. She consistently ditched school, became involved in drugs, was sexually active, and was generally irresponsible and belligerent, especially toward her stepfather.

Her fights with her stepfather became so bitter that she elected to move in with her father. There she began to fall apart. Formerly a beautiful girl with angelic features, blue eyes, blonde hair, and a lovely figure, she gained thirty pounds, let her hair grow ragged, and became increasingly depressed. Last year her mother finally persuaded her, at fifteen, to enter a psychiatric hospital.

'I took her to the hospital because she was getting so depressed. She had been depressed all her life, but I didn't really think it was a serious thing before. I just thought she'd outgrow it. I thought it was ordinary shyness, because I was shy.

'One day her doctor called me in and said, "I have something to tell you, but I want you to promise not to do anything about it without Alison's permission." Then he told me that Don had come in and admitted the incest to Alison's therapist. Don must have known that it would come out if she was in therapy, so he decided that things would go easier for him if he confessed.

'It seems that he had this ritual that he had performed with both the girls. When each one was five he began fondling their genitals and getting them to fondle him. Then he broke them in on oral sex. When each girl was fourteen he'd initiated them into intercourse. Kelly described it to me in great detail. He took the girls camping when she was fourteen, and he decided that this was the time when she should have genital intercourse. He used his finger to try and stretch the hymen, and it really made her feel gross – she hated it. And then he had intercourse and she remembers getting very sick. I remember her coming back from that trip. She was still sick, and had lost ten or fifteen pounds.

'I remember when we were together and the girls were just babies, we were discussing sex in general terms, which he often did, and he would bring up other societies and cultures and talk about the fact that our kids, boys and girls, don't have any practice, they don't know anything about sex. He said that girls ought to have experience with sex when they're teenagers. Of course he didn't tell me that he thought the father ought to be involved in that. It never entered my mind that he thought he should take on that responsibility.

'So he continued to have sex with the girls. Kelly pretty much put a stop to it when she was fifteen. She just refused to have anything physical to do with him, and I think she just turned away from men altogether. But Alison seemed to enjoy it a bit, at least at first. When she went to live with him one of the terms, apparently, was that she have sex with him. She apparently thought that was a good enough bargain to make to get away from under William, who is very strict. After a while, as I understand it, she began charging Don money for various sexual acts.

'After I found out about all this it was like the whole world just collapsed on me. There was this big empty space and I was floating around in no-man's land. My whole relationship with the children, I realized, was based on faulty premises. I was the odd man out. And my relationship with Don ... Even though there were eventually a lot of problems in our relationship, when it all started there wasn't the slightest indication to me that anything was wrong. We had no communication.

'So when Alison's doctor told me about the incest I was shocked. But he made me promise not to report anything for the sake of her therapy. He felt – and I think he was right – that Alison had to come to the decision to prosecute herself. A lot of her therapy was geared toward that. There were two things she could do – she could be quiet or she could report him. If she was quiet, what was she going to do with her anger? She could become self-destructive and suicidal, which I could see was her pattern, and she could crack up a car or hurt somebody else or something. Or she could become a lesbian like Kelly, and just turn away from it all. Or she could turn her anger on Don, which is where it belonged.

'What happened was that she didn't want to face it all, so she ran away. The doctor told me not to worry, that this always happens, and that she'd turn up, so I refused to let the normal pictures dominate my mind – that she'd run off and gotten killed or done something terrible. As it turned out she was hiding out in friends' houses. After a week I started worrying, so I called around. Of course no one would admit to knowing where she was, but sure enough, the next day she called. She wanted to come home, but William wouldn't have her. She refused to go back into the hospital, and I didn't want to force her into that because she'd just keep running away. So she went to Don's mother's house. She still couldn't make up her mind about prosecuting.

'I remember driving in the car with her one day. She was sitting next to me just being depressed, and both of us were feeling awful. I just kept yammering at her about what a bastard Don is, and how he's sick, and how he's so evil. She turned to me after a while and said, "I believe in the devil and I think my dad is the devil." I believe it too. He looks like the devil, he's so ugly! I can't even bear to look at him anymore. I'd like to kill him, I really would. How could he? These were my babies! There are times when I have gone out into the yard with my shears and I've just chopped bushes, and I could physically see his penis there being chopped off, time after time after time.

'During this whole time I just managed to keep myself going by pure will, by not letting that horrible anger get a hold of me too much. I kept feeling that I would disintegrate, I was just floating. Every once in a while I'd burst into tears, for no reason. I'd be sitting at the table or something, and this flood of feelings would come in and I'd just be sobbing.

'He was such a bastard, yet from all outward appearances he was a respectable man. I mean he's a high school teacher and all. I couldn't believe he was walking around free. But Alison didn't want to prosecute. She didn't want to send her dad to jail.

'Then she started telling me about how she hated her grandmother. Every time her grandmother started lecturing her about the way she was keeping her room or about the way she dressed Alison held in her anger, but I could see it wasn't going to work. I pointed out to Alison that this anger wasn't so much against her grandmother as against Don, or against herself. I told her she's got to put this anger somewhere, but where?

'Finally, one day she decided to do it, to prosecute. So I picked her up from school – we did all this behind her grandmother's back because we didn't want her to die of a heart attack.

'This was in May. The police were sensitive. They were kind to her and understanding.

'The next morning, though, she called me up and said, "I've decided not to prosecute." She had a boyfriend at the school near her grandmother's, and she wanted to stay there. I was really angry. It was obvious that Don had gone over and talked to her. "You've had your satisfaction," she said, and I could see that somehow he had made *me* the enemy. He managed to do this for about two or three weeks, and I was completely ineffectual. I didn't know what to do.

'In the meantime it had been reported, and they wouldn't allow her to drop the charges. So we were all kind of wondering what was going to happen. Then the social workers found out where she was, and decided that it was an intolerable situation for her to be so accessible to her father, so they put her in another placement. They worked with her, and got her out from under his influence, and she finally decided to prosecute.'

The preliminary hearing was held in September. The purpose of this procedure was to determine whether there was sufficient evidence to bring the matter before a jury. The rules of evidence and the courtroom procedure were identical to those that would follow in a trial if the judge found sufficient cause to hold the matter over. Alison, then sixteen, was the first witness. After she was sworn in the prosecuting attorney directed her attention to Don, who was seated at the defense table. The following exchange is from the transcript of the hearing:

Prosecution: I want to direct your attention first of all to the gentleman seated at the end of the counsel table. Are you in some way related to him?

Alison: Yes. He's my father.

Defense: Objection. Hearsay.

The Court: Well, the mother can testify to that.

Prosecution: I'm certain by this age, she ought to know.

Defense: Your Honor, she has no first-hand knowledge.

The Court: All right. Sustained.

The objection to Alison referring to Don as her father was sustained throughout the trial. She testified for about five hours before her mother was sworn in to clear up the matter of her parentage. After Karen testified that Don was indeed Alison's father she was cross-examined.

Defense: Did you have Alison by natural childbirth?

Karen: No.

Defense: Were you sedated at the time of the delivery?

Karen: I had a Cesarean section.

Defense: Then, am I correct in assuming that you were under some type of anesthesia from the time you went into the hospital ...

The Court: If there could be such a thing, it's very remote that there was a mixup of babies, but I'm not going to hold that that would be enough to set aside – I think that's too remote. Where anything is possible, there could be a mixup.

There followed a legal argument between the attorneys as to whether a mother can identify her baby if it is born while she is under anesthesia. Such peripheral arguments dominated the hearing.

More than twenty pages of transcript were taken up with attempts by both the prosecution and the defense to pin Alison down to a specific incident of incest on a specific date. Yet she made it very clear at the outset that she could remember a specific incident, but that she could not tie it down to a date. A typical exchange:

> *Defense:* Alison, on what day between April 1st and April 15th of 1976 did any of the sexual relationships that you described in your direct testimony occur?
>
> *Alison:* I can't be sure.
>
> *Defense:* Can you be sure that any of them occurred on the first day of April 1976?
>
> *Alison:* No.
>
> *Defense:* The second day?
>
> *Alison:* No.
>
> *Defense:* Any of the following days up through the 15th, can you pick a day when any of these occurrences ...?
>
> *Alison:* Do you want me to pick a day?
>
> *Defense:* A day upon which your testimony was based that these matters occurred between you and the defendant.
>
> *Alison:* Okay. If you want me to pick, I'll take 7.
>
> *Defense:* I want you to pick a day upon which things occurred.
>
> *The Court:* I think she has indicated she can't pick a day.

The testimony Alison was required to give regarding exactly what took place between herself and her father was particularly humiliating. She was forced to go into precise, graphic description of every action, every organ, every contact – and this before a courtroom of strangers. She was forced to belabor the details of how she began to extract money from her father for her sexual favors. At this point the defense counsel attempted to intimidate her even further by alleging that she might be opening herself up to prosecution for prostitution:

> *Defense:* Your Honor, in a dual role as officer of the court, I have to at least raise my feelings about whether this witness has

been apprised of her rights regarding possible self-incrimination.

Prosecution: I'll waive any advisement by the court on her behalf, if I can. If Counsel is suggesting that she may be charged with prostitution, I'm perfectly willing to say that that's not the case, she being of an age [fifteen at the time of the offense] where she cannot consent legally and consent being no issue, therefore.

The Court: I don't think at this point that the Court would say it would serve any purpose to advise her.

Defense: As long as there would be no chance that a witness would draw a conclusion by the District Attorney's oral statement that there would be no prosecution.

Prosecution: I think it's perfectly appropriate for her to draw such a conclusion.

A good deal of the hearing could have been written by Lewis Carroll, for indeed there was a Wonderlandish quality about many of the legal arguments. The defense attorney bore in on Alison, asking her to remember what people were wearing on specific dates, what magazines she remembered seeing in the house, whom she visited during the week of the alleged offense, whom she talked to, etc. By the end of the afternoon she was exhausted and exasperated:

Defense: Do you seem to have a pretty good memory for facts, Alison?

Alison: No, I don't.

Defense: Do facts irritate you in some manner?

Alison: You do.

Defense: I don't think that's responsive to the question.

The Court: All right. We will strike her comment about what you do to her.

Prosecution: That's an idiotic question, your Honor. I object to the question. 'Do facts normally irritate you?' Is that an intelligent question? I think the answer was responsive, your Honor.

Defense: It has to be stretched to make that responsive.

Prosecution: He asked in some manner and she is explaining in what manner.

Defense: If I'm a fact, I imagine so. I don't question my own existence, but I guess we all do.

The Court: Well, I'll leave it in for what it's worth. I think it's sort of argumentative, and you kind of evoke such an answer.

Defense: Alison, does it irritate you to have me ask questions that ask you for specific things that were being worn or people you talked to on the occasion of the oral copulation here?

Alison: In the manner that you ask them to me, yes. I'm awfully muddle-headed right now. It's been a long day sitting in this chair, and my feet are freezing. It seems like awful trivia.

The Court: She said she feels they're trivial. I think that answers it.

The defense managed to confuse Alison into making quite a few minor inconsistencies in her testimony, but the court took into account the natural confusion that any witness would fall victim to under such double-spoken badgering, so the defendant was held over for trial.

As this book goes to press Don is awaiting a trial date. Alison, wiser for her experience during the hearing, is again having second thoughts about prosecuting, but I think she will go ahead with the trial. After the hearing I asked her what she hopes will happen to her father.

'I'd like him to get long-term psychiatric care,' she said. Then she laughed, and added, 'That will make him suffer enough. I don't want him to go to jail; I don't want to break his spirit.'

I asked her why she had put up with the incestuous relationship for so long.

'I had this really overpowering fear that my father would retaliate. Now I feel really guilty that I'm the reason he is having all this trouble. You know, he ran to my doctor – oh, that was another thing. I hate men, right? So the first thing they do is stick me with this asshole male psychiatrist who asks me if I hear voices. I mean after everything that's happened all he's interested in is if I hear voices! So my dad went and confessed to my doctor when he heard I was in therapy, like a little kid defending himself. He thought it would go easier with him if he confessed.

'I feel like I'm about 85 percent damaged. All the fun I had as a little kid came from the things Dad taught me, like my interest in nature and animals. But in order to get his involvement I had to put out. So I was like a prostitute: I'd make him happy so he'd do things with me. I'm really pissed at my mom for not realizing what was going on and protecting me. I can't ever trust anybody again. My relationships with men and women are really bad. With men I just pick them up and put them down – I'm angry at them all. I would like to be close to someone, but I can't. I get rid of them fast so I won't be close.'

Torn by her own conflicts, Alison found the decision to prosecute a difficult one to make. But she came to grips with the decision, and is presently working in treatment on her conflicts. Despite the fact that she is doing well in her present foster placement and treatment program, Alison is still struggling with guilt about what may happen to her father. She hates him, but becomes overwhelmed with feelings of sadness and loss when she recalls the good times they had when she was younger. With all she's undergone she still has to suffer through at least two more courtroom proceedings during which she will be humiliated, degraded, badgered, and confused.

Alison – again like the rape victim of a few years ago – was treated like a criminal instead of a victim in court. During her trial she was accused of various drug offenses, of prostitution, of extortion, of seducing her father, of wild promiscuity, and of incorrigibility. Despite the fact that her father had confessed the incest to Alison's psychiatrist the defense attorney tried to establish that the incest might have been an hallucination on her part rather than a reality. When Alison left the courtroom after the hearing she looked like she had completed a rigorous physical workout.

The hearing was also an ordeal for Alison's mother. Her testimony was brief and confined to identifying Don as Alison's father, but during the rest of the hearing she was excluded from the courtroom. Thus she sat alone outside the court, worrying about her daughter, hating her ex-husband, and wondering where she had gone wrong. The entire incest experience shook her confidence; she is seeking psychiatric help for the first time in her life to help her cope.

Don seemed unperturbed in court, but then he didn't have to testify. The courtroom proceedings typically revolved around legal technicalities at Alison's expense. (Considering every defendant's right to a good legal defense the questions raised by such legal maneuverings admittedly do not lend themselves to easy answers.)

Alison voiced an important issue when she stated that she did not want her father to be imprisoned. Instead she wanted him to be forced into treatment (though I think, in this case, he should also be prevented from continuing to work with children as a teacher, at least until the court judges him rehabilitated). I spoke with more than three dozen judges, commissioners, lawyers, police officers, social workers, district attorneys, county counsels, and psychologists about this form of sentencing, and their responses were virtually identical: Incest aggressors, unless they demonstrate some abnormal tendency toward violence, should generally be sentenced to treatment rather than prison.

I commend their judgment. Therapeutic sentencing would not only help aggressors resolve their conflicts, but it might also serve to reunite some families – the breakdown of which, after all, is one of the things the law is meant to prevent.

INCEST AND THE LAW IN THE UNITED KINGDOM

In the United Kingdom incest by a man is defined as having 'sexual intercourse with a woman whom he knows to be his granddaughter, daughter, sister or mother' (the consent of the woman is immaterial). Incest by a woman of the age of sixteen or over is defined as permitting 'a man whom she knows to be her grandfather, father, brother or son to have sexual intercourse with her by her consent' (Section 10 and 11 of the Sexual Offences Act 1956).

Under the Marriage Act 1949 the degrees of consanguinity within which marriages are void are wider than for incestuous relationships. Thus some people are prevented from marrying although any sexual relationship between them is not incestuous unless they come within the above definitions.

The liability for the offense of incest is not absolute as it must be proved that the accused was aware of the relationship at the time. The penalty for incest is a maximum of seven years' imprisonment. If, however, incest is committed by a man with a girl who, at the time of the offense, is under thirteen then the maximum is life imprisonment. An attempt to commit the offense is also punishable with imprisonment for not more than two years. Further it is an offense for a man to incite a girl under the age of sixteen whom he knows to be his granddaughter, daughter or sister to have sexual intercourse with him and the punishment is a maximum of two years' imprisonment.

There is an irrefutable presumption that a boy under the age of fourteen is incapable of performing sexual intercourse.

If a person is convicted of incest against a girl or boy under the age of eighteen, he or she may be divested of all authority over the child.

13 · LEARNING TO TRUST AGAIN

Throughout this book we have examined the dynamics of incest – the underlying causes, motivations, and interactions that combine to create overt sexuality within the family. We have seen that incest is generally the effect, not the cause, of fragmented family relationships. And we have seen many of the symptoms of incest – migraines, depression, self-hatred, drug addiction, alcoholism, promiscuity, impotence, prostitution, violence, an inability to trust or be close, and homosexuality.

Over the past ten years I have treated several hundred incest victims and aggressors. Their ages have ranged from thirteen to sixty. I have treated them in psychiatric hospitals, outpatient therapy, and private practice, in group, family, and individual therapy. My goal with these patients has been to help them gain the courage to reveal the incest and to encourage them to work the experience and its accompanying guilt out of their unconscious so that their conflicts can be revealed, understood, and resolved.

I am frequently asked how I can tolerate the emotional strain of working with such an intense, painful subject as incest. The work is undeniably draining for me, especially since my therapeutic style is to be very active and involved with the patient, but the rewards are enormous. I am constantly replenished by the dramatic relief of symptoms and changes in behavior that I see in my patients once they have purged themselves of their terrible secret.

Therapy works well for the vast majority of my patients: Their headaches decrease or disappear, their depression recedes, many become orgasmic for the first time, they learn to like themselves, and as a result they develop self-confidence which permits them to trust people and form close relationships – possibly for the first time in their lives. It is these successes that keep me going.

The form of treatment I have found most effective with incest is group therapy. Patients enter my therapy groups in response to a wide range of conflicts and symptoms; still, about 20 percent of my patients reveal incestuous experiences during therapy. Many of these people had been in individual therapy previously, yet had not been able to shed their sense of shame and disclose the incest. Both victims and aggressors feel isolated and freakish, as if, of the world's population, they alone have been involved in incest. In group therapy, however, they discover that other people have had similar experiences, and that we all have done things in our lives that we are ashamed of, things that make us feel guilty. The group provides an atmosphere of nurturing and support in which the incest victim or aggressor often finds the courage for the first time to discuss the incestuous experience. This type of supportiveness is unique to group therapy, and makes it ideal for working with hidden traumas like incest.

Since incest is so often the result of a family breakdown family therapy might appear to be the most effective method of treatment. But in many situations family therapy is impossible, or even undesirable. Often the incest has occurred so long ago that participating family members may have died, be geographically dispersed, or simply uncooperative. In situations where the incest is recent the family may be so badly fragmented emotionally that they must first be treated individually, so that each member can learn to cope with his or her own incest guilts and responsibilities. Only after the aggressor and the silent partner have accepted their responsibility, and the victim has accepted the fact that he or she has none, can the family be successfully treated together.

Some patients, however, require the constant care found in one-to-one therapy, and others are simply unable to tolerate the therapeutic interaction with their family or with a group. The choice of a method of treatment must be based on the specific needs of each individual patient.

Whatever form of treatment is chosen there are two inevitable therapeutic steps that every incest patient must take on the path to psychological health. First he or she must be willing to make a considerable commitment to treatment. Psychotherapy is not like conventional medicine, where the patient essentially does no more than describe symptoms, then passively allow the doctor to administer treatment.

In psychotherapy the patient must do more work than the therapist – and it is hard work, often frightening. Digging deeply into the unconscious and exposing previously repressed feelings, thoughts, wishes, and fantasies is a painful and anxiety-provoking process. It takes time, effort, and endurance of emotional stress.

And second, once the patient has made the commitment to treatment, he or she must be willing to face the incest, to admit that it has taken place. Lifelong patterns of secrecy and repression are difficult to break. Though some patients are able to talk about their incestuous experiences early in therapy many others need time and constant reassurance before they are able to open up. All of my patients have wanted to rid themselves of their incest secret, but few have known how to go about doing it, so they tend to drop hints about the incest along the way, like bits of bait, enticing me to draw their stories from them.

Once I suspect incest to have occurred in a patient with whom I have established a trusting relationship a gentle question will usually be enough to reveal it – a question like, 'You know, a lot of people with your symptoms have had sexual experiences they feel guilty about; has anything like that ever happened to you?'

Sometimes the answers can be pretty blunt. I'll never forget a baby-faced blonde girl of fifteen, who was in one of my adolescent groups. She had been talking about what a 'creep' her stepfather was and I asked her if he'd ever gotten fresh with her. She told us that he had tried molesting her once when he was drunk. 'What happened?' I asked. 'He told me to suck it; I told him to shove it,' she said.

I revealed my own incest very reluctantly during the first session I had with my psychiatrist a number of years ago. I entered therapy at twenty-eight because my marriage was breaking up. At first I talked at great length about my marital difficulties, but in the back of my mind I knew that I would eventually have to reveal the incestuous relationship with my father, though I had hidden it for thirteen years. I became increasingly tense until finally I blurted the story out. I felt a great release.

The doctor nodded slowly. 'That's where you were traumatized,' he said. 'Girls should never have their fantasies of possessing daddy come true – it's too frightening for them.' He had heard me; he had understood; and he didn't think I was awful! I recall a surge of relief and gratitude coming over me.

Revealing a major trauma and venting feelings is just the beginning of the therapeutic process. But people sometimes find so much relief in that initial revelation of incest, and in being accepted by the therapy group despite that revelation, that they leave treatment prematurely, thinking they are 'cured.' This is known as a 'flight into health' – a short flight. When the initial euphoria wears off the patient is still struggling with unresolved conflicts. I always warn my patients that emotional purgings need to be experienced repeatedly if guilt is to be effectively worn away.

Once the incest is revealed and the commitment to treatment has been made I draw from a variety of psychological disciplines for my treatment techniques, depending on the particular needs of the patient. I generally intersperse these techniques with psychodrama – or role-playing – a powerful treatment method that offers the opportunity to explore and resolve conflicts by acting them out in brief, improvised scenes. I have found psychodrama to be the most effective means of working with the incest trauma. Psychodrama cuts through the intellectualizing and denial that many patients use as a defense against their feelings; it offers patients a chance to express their feelings toward family members, perhaps for the first time, without fear; and it provides a safe atmosphere in which to try out new behaviors. All three factors are essential to successful treatment.

Psychodrama sometimes also serves as a rehearsal for real-life confrontations, helping patients gain self-confidence and assertiveness. Frequently the enacted confrontation is sufficient for patients to work out their feelings, but some patients feel a need to confront their betrayers in actuality. Only the patient can decide whether the confrontation need be real or role-played.

WORKING WITH THE VICTIM

In using psychodrama with incest victims I attempt to achieve three goals. First I attempt to get the patient to externalize the guilt, rage, shame, hurt, fear, and confusion that have been bottled up inside. Without this externalization the patient is fighting an invisible enemy.

The second goal is to help the victim place the responsibility for the incest firmly where it belongs – primarily with the aggressor, and to a lesser extent with the silent partner. Placing the responsibility where it belongs – with the adult – is vital to helping the victim renounce her own feelings of responsibility. (Because seven out of eight victims are female and the corresponding number of aggressors are male, for ease of reading I will use 'she' and 'he' throughout this chapter in referring to victims and aggressors respectively.)

The third goal is to teach the patient that although significant damage has been done to her dignity and sense of self-worth she does not have to be psychologically crippled for the rest of her life. I encourage my patients to invest the same energy they have been putting into self-destructive behavior into self-fulfilling behavior.

In a typical session with an incest victim, group members – including myself – will play the various figures in the patient's life, giving her an opportunity to express a broad spectrum of long-concealed feelings. I ask her to address each family member one at a time, beginning with her father, then her mother, then whoever else may be involved – brothers, sisters, uncles, etc. The patient need not go into the sexual details of the incest: Her feelings about what happened are the major focus of treatment. Even though the people to whom these feelings are directed may not actually be present, patients seem to quickly forget they are confronting substitute relatives. The role-played scenes are almost always very real and powerful to both the patients and the group. The best way to understand how psychodrama works is to look at a few excerpts from my groups.

Rena Sommers

The first case is based on a recent session with twenty-seven-year-old Rena Sommers, who had been repeatedly molested by her grandfather when she was eleven.

Rena had told her mother about her grandfather's sexual assault immediately after it had first occurred. Her mother had told her there wasn't anything she could do about it because: 'We can't upset Grandpa; you know what a weak heart he has. Just try to stay away from him.'

As a result of the incest Rena's adolescent and adult life had been chaotic. She was finally hospitalized after years of severe depression and multiple suicide attempts.

A week before the therapy session I am about to describe Rena's grandfather had died. She had refused to attend the funeral. This left her feeling very unfinished, because her relationship with her grandfather had never been resolved.

I decided to work with Rena's unresolved relationship in group that week. When one of the characters in a psychodrama scene is dead I frequently use an empty chair to symbolize that person, rather than using a living individual. This is the technique I used with Rena. I asked her to face an empty chair and say 'goodbye' to her grandfather.

As she spoke she wept: 'I loved you and I hated you ... I don't know how you could have done that to a little girl ... at least now you can't hurt me anymore ... but I'll miss the good times we had ... goodbye ...'

In those few sentences Rena expressed the terrible push and tug of conflicting feelings that are so typical of incest victims. There was no ambivalence, however, in the next part of her work, when she asked me to play her mother – I had a hunch about what was coming.

'You bitch!' she screamed. 'Why didn't you stop him? You were my mother – you were supposed to protect me! How could you choose him over me?'

Rena's long repressed anger at her mother was finally out in the open. She could begin to deal with the sad reality of her mother's inability to nurture and shield her. She could start to resolve her guilt over having such anger toward the people she was supposed to love – anger that had been turned inward, against herself, becoming depression. I pointed out to Rena that her suicide attempt could be seen as an unconscious wish to murder those who had betrayed her, but because that wish was so laden with guilt she had chosen instead to 'murder' herself. She seemed to understand, and her general mood improved.

Today Rena is no longer in the hospital, but she still attends outpatient groups several times a week. She remains somewhat disturbed – her sense of guilt is still strong – but she is improving steadily.

Nicole James

Feelings of guilt and responsibility also caused great conflict for Nicole James, whose case we examined in the victim chapter. After being abused by her brothers Nicole had been beaten by her father for having her clothes off. A few years later she sought relief from her brothers' continued abuse by confiding in her uncle. He, in turn, molested her. With no nurturing or support from anyone close to her Nicole learned early to despise and blame herself for the incest.

I had worked with Nicole for over a year both in the hospital and in outpatient therapy, and I was concerned over her relentlessly self-destructive behavior. She spoke frequently of just wanting to die. I decided to become directive, to structure her work so that she might feel, if only for a few minutes, what it would be like to free herself from the guilt she had lived with all her life.

Nicole had admitted her incest to the group, but still insisted that it had been her own responsibility. 'Listen, Nicole,' I said. 'I want you to tell your mother that it wasn't your fault. You really need to get in touch with that message loud and clear, because you blame yourself for everything you didn't do.'

'How can I say something that's not true?' she asked. 'I think it's 100 percent my fault. I did it.'

'I want you to try it from the stance that it was not your fault,' I said. 'Come on . . . just to see how it feels. Let's get down to work on this. I'll be your mother.'

The psychodrama began:

Susan (as Nicole's mother): Nicole, you always get yourself into these terrible situations where something happens and then you come crying to us and it's too late. What were we supposed to do about it?

Nicole (after a long pause): I guess the reason why I was there was because you never gave me love, the love that I needed.

Susan (as Nicole's mother): What is she talking about, that we never gave her love? What kind of crazy stuff is that? Didn't we feed you, didn't we clothe you? You're so ungrateful. You've always been so ungrateful. What do you want out of life? What do you want?

Nicole (after another long pause she screams her reply): I just want to be held! I just want to be held!

Susan (as Nicole's mother): You may never get that from us.

Nicole (she pulls herself into a ball and begins to cry).

Susan: Do you want to be held right now?

Nicole (she faintly nods her assent).

Susan (embracing Nicole): Yes, I think you do. It's all right, Nicole. It wasn't your fault. Your brothers forced you to do what you did. And your uncle exploited your need for love. It wasn't your fault. (Nicole clutches at Susan, greedy for contact.)

That scene was pivotal in Nicole's treatment. She understood for the first time that what had happened had been done *to* her, she had not brought it on herself. Her guilt did not magically disappear with that realization, but the way was cleared to work on it.

The following session found Nicole considerably more courageous and able to confront her uncle in a psychodrama scene – a big step for her. Another group member played the part of her uncle:

John (as Nicole's uncle): Nicole, I don't understand why you're so upset. We were having such a wonderful time.

Nicole: Wonderful time?

John: Yes. For four years you were my wife. I loved you like a wife.

Nicole: I was never your wife. I just did what I did because I had to. It was like a duty.

John: You were replacing my wife.

Nicole: Everybody always figured they could walk all over me. 'Good old Nicole. She won't complain. She'll do anything she can to please everybody. She'll be there for us. Good old Nicole.' I told you I wanted to stop, that I couldn't stand it any longer. My God, you almost drove me totally insane! I swallowed a whole bottle of pills; I drank a whole bottle of liquor. I damn near died, and you got mad because they wanted to put me in a psych ward. You're the one that stopped me from getting the psychiatric care I needed five years ago. You talked my parents out of putting me in that psychiatric hospital where I needed to be.

John: But you needed to be with me.

Nicole: No, I didn't. I never did.

John: But I loved you, Nicole. And I respected you.

Nicole: Respect! You call that respect?

John: With all my heart I loved you.

Nicole: You should have loved me as a niece, not as a lover.

As I pointed out in the victim chapter Nicole still has a distance to go before her symptoms will recede enough to allow her to lead a normal life. But she is moving in the right direction.

It is when patients actually begin to change their destructive behavior that my work becomes especially fulfilling. This occurred in the following case.

Ethel James

Ethel James changed her life patterns drastically, even though she was well into middle age. Ethel was fifty-five when I met her. She was depressed, suicidal, obese, and suffering from chronic migraines.

For several weeks Ethel talked about her 'empty nest' – her last child had gotten married and now Ethel had no purpose in life. She had lived only to serve and care for others; her own wishes and needs were unimportant to her. Her husband was cold and distant, her children were gone, and her life was hopeless.

I decided to let Ethel work at her own pace in group, to see what would develop. One day she told us that she felt 'unclean – dirtier than anyone in the world.' When I asked why she felt that way she buried her face in her hands and began to sob.

She told us that she had been molested when she was six by her uncle – a priest who was a great source of pride for her religious, French-Catholic family. She had been terrified, bewildered. She told her parents about the molestation, but they reacted in disbelief. How could she have such wicked ideas about her pious uncle? They called her a 'little whore,' and unknowingly reinforced the guilt that would plague her for the next fifty years.

In group, during the next several months, we gave Ethel ample opportunity to express her guilt and anguish. She began to improve noticeably – her headaches receded, her depression lessened, and she even went on a diet. Then one day she came into group and announced that she had enrolled in a master's program in languages at a local university.

I asked her how she had managed to be accepted so quickly. 'Well,' she said, 'I graduated *magna cum laude* many years ago ...' The group was astonished at this unexpected admission. 'How come you never told us?' I asked.

'I didn't think it was important,' she replied. 'My parents didn't even come to my graduation. They were upset that I hadn't become a nun, like they wanted me to.' In group that day, for perhaps the first time in her life, she felt proud of her academic abilities. And the fact that she was going back to school showed that she believed in them – and in herself.

Ethel's renewed self-confidence was not the only change. She also became more trusting and open toward other people. When she had first started therapy I had noticed that she did not like to be touched or to touch others. Since I often touch my patients to reassure them during especially emotional sessions I asked Ethel about her aversion. She told me she had 'the touch of death.' She went on to explain that when she was a child it was a family custom to bring the children into the room of a dying relative. The children were told to kiss and hug the dying person as a way of saying goodbye. Ethel associated her embrace with the person's subsequent death, feeling responsible for it. In her mind touching and death were intertwined, and she came to believe that her touch was deadly.

One day I told her I wanted her to hug each group member so that she would see that her belief was a superstition. I volunteered to go first. She was genuinely frightened of the exercise, and went through the motions unwillingly, mechanically. But by the time she had hugged three or four people she began to relax. Soon she was smiling and embracing group members warmly. 'If anyone dies tomorrow, remember: I warned you,' she said, laughing. From then on she began each session by hugging everyone in the room.

The warmth and humor that sometimes occurs in groups is wonderfully therapeutic.

WORKING WITH THE AGGRESSOR AND THE SILENT PARTNER

In working with aggressors (usually fathers or stepfathers) and silent partners the focus of treatment shifts. Where the victim must renounce responsibility the aggressor (and, to a lesser extent, the silent partner) must accept it. Though most aggressors feel considerable guilt over what they have done they often try to minimize their role and exaggerate the victim's seductiveness and willing participation. The incestuous father also tends to blame his wife for her neglect of him, suggesting that she, too, is to blame for the incest.

All of this denial and projection of guilt onto others must be confronted in treatment before constructive changes can begin to take place. The aggressor must come to the realization that he, and he alone, was responsible for permitting the act to occur. No matter how much the situation was set up by the victim and the silent partner it was he who took advantage of it.

The threat of losing his family is often a powerful motivation for the aggressor to stay in treatment, with or without pressure from the legal system. The silent partner, on the other hand, often uses the same denial and emotional neglect that have contributed so significantly to the incest to deny her need to be involved in the treatment process. She will typically back out of therapy by saying something like, 'I didn't do anything. Why should I be treated?' Her self-esteem has been shattered by the experience, and she tends to view herself as a victim. She evades facing both her part in a nongratifying marriage and her rivalry with her daughter. In my experience the mothers who are most strongly motivated to participate in treatment are those who either had no role in the incest or were active participants.

In working with aggressors and victims' mothers I still find psychodrama to be the most effective technique. Through role-playing the aggressor may understand for the first time how traumatic the incest experience was for the victim, though he may have previously supposed her to be a willing participant. The silent partner may realize for the first time how she has let the victim down. These realizations are illustrated well in the following case.

The Dane Family

Paul Dane is a short, obese, shoe salesman. He married an eighteen-year-old girl when he was twenty-three because he had gotten her pregnant. Their relationship was stormy from the beginning, and when their daughter Diane was born the added burden estranged Paul and his wife even further.

When Diane was five Paul began molesting her. Two years later he initiated intercourse, and continued until Diane was thirteen. Then she began seeing boys her own age.

Paul became extremely jealous of these young suitors – a very common reaction of incest aggressors – and tried to restrict Diane's socializing by constantly criticizing her friends and 'grounding' her frequently. Incest often comes to light because the victim cannot withstand the pressure of the aggressor's oppressive jealousy. This pressure eventually became too much for Diane, and she admitted the incest to a teacher she trusted at school. Paul was arrested that evening.

Paul was ordered by the court to enter therapy. A few weeks later he was joined by his wife: 'Paul tells me you don't take any crap from anybody,' she said, 'so I thought I'd better come in too and see if we can't straighten out our relationship.'

I was also treating Diane, though separately. I worked with the Danes in individual therapy, rather than in a group, because all three refused to talk about the incest with others.

With Paul my goal was to get him to accept not only his responsibility for the incest, but the fact that it had been traumatic to Diane.

'Okay, so it was wrong,' he said. 'But it's over and done with. Diane's all right. She's doing okay in school. Our relationship was loving. She did it because she wanted to, she liked it. It was our way of loving each other.'

In working with Diane it became clear that she was *not* 'all right.' She confided to me that not only was she compulsively promiscuous in her social relationships, but at the same time she found sex revolting. 'I slept with all those boys because I needed the loving,' she said, 'but I hated it.'

Without violating confidentiality I tried to persuade Paul through role-playing that Diane was damaged by the incest, but he would not believe that I was really expressing Diane's feelings. Finally I arranged for Diane to join her parents in therapy. She did not seem to feel threatened by her parents, so I felt she could handle family treatment. I wanted Paul to understand that Diane's perception of the incest was far different from what he thought it was. I accomplished this by asking Diane to do a psychodrama scene in which I would play her, and she would play her father:

> *Susan* (as Diane): How could you have sex with your own daughter? How could you do that to me?

Diane   (as Paul): I wanted to have sex with somebody, and you were around.

Susan   (as Diane): You mean you didn't love me?

Diane   (as Paul): Is that your idea of love – screwing your own daughter? I used you, that's all. Nobody loves you.

Susan   (as Diane): How can you say that? I know you love me, I could feel it when you touched me.

Diane   (as Paul): That was just sex.

Susan   (as Diane): What about mom? She loves me.

Diane   (as Paul): If she loved you so much she would have protected you.

Susan   (as Diane): How?

Diane   (as Paul): I don't know. She just would have that's all.

Diane and her mother started crying, at which point Paul said, 'I can't believe it. Diane, how could you think I didn't love you? Oh my God, I thought ... all this time ... I really don't know what to say. I just never dreamed ... you seemed to like it ...'

And Diane answered, 'I just wanted you to love me. That's all I want from anybody.'

From that day on the family therapy went very well. Both Paul and his wife learned to accept their respective responsibility for the incest, and Diane learned that she was more than just an object for someone else's sexual gratification. Her social life, which had been devoted primarily to a series of short-lived sexual relationships with older boys, settled into more stable, somewhat restrained relationships with her peers.

I am still working with the Dane family; they have been in treatment for over a year. I believe they have rehabilitated themselves. The marriage is on much firmer ground as a result of their having talked out their differences for the first time in therapy. And Diane has resolved her conflicts with both her parents through much the same process. Through psychodrama and subsequent discussions the family members have come to understand each other's thoughts and feelings.

Diane is presently living in a foster placement, but I have testified on behalf of her parents before the court in hopes of reuniting the family.

Psychologically I think they are ready to live together again, though the court has yet to agree.

INCEST AND THE THERAPIST

Despite the enormous benefits that the incest patient can derive from the psychotherapeutic process, incest is one of those topics that some therapists shy away from for reasons of their own – much to the detriment of their patients. There are three general reasons for this tendency: personal discomfort with the subject, little training in incest treatment, and a psychoanalytic tradition that for many years regarded incest reports as fantasies rather than actualities.

Personal conflicts are not unusual for a therapist. We are just as vulnerable to stress as anyone else. But a competent, experienced therapist should be able to keep his or her personal difficulties outside the therapeutic relationship. Often a therapist will feel uneasy about a patient's report of incest because it stirs up the therapist's own Oedipal conflicts or possibly even an incestuous experience. Male therapists may identify with the aggressor unconsciously, becoming subtly hostile and accusatory toward the victim. Female therapists may identify with the victim, unconsciously reliving their own incest conflicts and tending to avoid dealing with the topic, as I did when I first ran into incest.

Several years ago, when I was a graduate student in psychiatric social work, I was assigned for part of my internship to a community crisis clinic. One of my first patients was a young actress named Joan Meredith. She was suffering severe depression. I was to work with Joan and tape-record our sessions so my supervisor could later review my work.

In one of our sessions, as Joan began to talk about her father, she suddenly broke down and told me about sexual advances he had made when she was thirteen. When I replayed the tape for my supervisor later that day I was horrified to discover that when Joan had brought up the incest my reaction had been to change the subject. I had jumped in with an unrelated question without realizing it. My supervisor assured me that even some experienced therapists react the same way, but I was shaken. nonetheless. I had simply not been trained to deal with another person's incestuous conflicts.

Many therapists do not receive such training, either in terms of dealing with their own feelings or with their patients'. Incest education in medical schools and mental health graduate schools is almost nonexistent. And, ironically, many of those therapists who have received some incest training were taught the classical Freudian approach, which presents still another problem in dealing with incest.

In 1897 Freud wrote a letter to his friend and associate Wilhelm Fliess, in which he explained a chain of reasoning that brought him to conclude that almost all of the incest reports from his patients were fantasies: 'Then there was the astonishing thing that in every case blame was laid on perverse acts by the father ... though it was hardly credible that perverted acts against children were so general.' In essence, because Freud couldn't believe so much incest was going on, he assumed that it wasn't.

The pendulum is now swinging the other way. Therapists are beginning to realize that, unless there is strong evidence to the contrary, all incest reports should be considered valid.

I think the next five years will see a new, reasoned attitude toward incest, and an understanding of the social problems it presents: juvenile delinquency, alcoholism, drug abuse, prostitution, and violence, which can all be reduced if incest is dealt with in an open, informed, and sensitive manner.

The incest trauma has been plaguing mankind for thousands of years, but only now that it is being exposed to the light of understanding can we begin the task of reducing its consequences through new educational and treatment programs. More immediately, anyone who has been involved in incest can do something about the trauma *now* – through psychotherapy. Though introspection and self-confrontation are painful processes they are certainly more tolerable than a lifetime of emotional anguish. I know that the devastation of incest can be overcome. Hundreds of my patients have done it. I did it. So can others.

MORE ABOUT PENGUINS AND PELICANS

For further information about books available from
Penguins please write to Dept EP, Penguin Books Ltd,
Harmondsworth, Middlesex UB7 0DA.

In the U.S.A.: For a complete list of books available
from Penguins in the United States write to Dept CS,
Penguin Books, 625 Madison Avenue, New York, New York
10022.

In Canada: For a complete list of books available from
Penguins in Canada write to Penguin Books Canada Ltd,
2801 John Street, Markham, Ontario L3R 1B4.

In Australia: For a complete list of books available from
Penguins in Australia write to the Marketing Department,
Penguin Books Australia Ltd, PO Box 257, Ringwood,
Victoria 3134.

The Ambivalence of Abortion
Linda Bird Francke

A lucid and objective examination of one of the most controversial and complicated issues of our time. The author starts from the assumption that women have the right to choose and then looks at the consequences of that choice. In interviews with men and women of all ages and all social groups, she not only casts new light on the subject but also questions many of the emotional and sexual values of our society.

Baby and Child
Penelope Leach

A complete manual of baby and child care for parents and all those required to work with children, written by one of Britain's leading experts on the subject.

Boy, Girl, Man, Woman: A Guide to Sex for Young People
B. H. Claësson

A book devoted to the special needs of the young. Informative and sympathetic, it enables them to increase their sexual awareness and enjoy their own sexuality.

The Language of Madness
David Cooper

The language of madness, maintains David Cooper, expresses a radical need for change, and is an indictment of society's failure to recognize that need and of our corporate failure to bring together our sexuality, our lives and our autonomy. Cooper claims that we must accept this indictment and points to ways in which we can remedy the situation. He also restates the position that he, together with R. D. Laing, put forward on schizophrenia in the fifties and sixties: a statement that is now more forceful than ever. Finally Cooper concludes that the answer lies in taking madness out of a clinical context – which only represents repression and social control – to find its place in a world of universal creativity.

Make It Happy: What Sex is All About
Jane Cousins

'... seeks to dispel much irrationality in current thinking about sex. A book that should be in every teenager's library' – Dr Peter Jackson, National Council of the FPA

An honest, frank and encouraging book aimed particularly at the teenage market. Its doctrine is simply that sex is something to be shared, enjoyed and understood. It covers, among other things, how our bodies are built and how they function, masturbation, orgasm, virginity, birth control, abortion, having a baby, looking after our bodies, sex and the law.

The Piggle:
An Account of the Psychoanalytic Treatment of a Little Girl
D. W. Winnicott

Of special value to those who work with children, but also of interest to anyone involved with children, this account of the psychoanalytic treatment of a young child vividly illustrates the importance of psychoanalytic theory and technique in the understanding of children and childhood.

Treat Yourself to Sex: A Guide to Good Loving
Paul Brown and Carolyn Faulder

Basic, readable and sympathetic, this handbook deals with a range
of sexual problems that are more common than is generally supposed,
and gives a series of exercises – 'sexpieces' – worked out after extensive
research, which will help to provide workable solutions.

PSYCHOLOGY, PSYCHIATRY AND SOCIOLOGY – OTHER TITLES

The Divided Self R. D. Laing
The Grammar of Living David Cooper
Human Aggression Anthony Storr
*I, Pierre Rivière, Having Slaughtered My Mother, My Sister and
    My Brother: A Case of Parricide in the Nineteenth Century*
    Edited by Michael Foucault
The Moral Judgement of the Child Jean Piaget
The New Sex Therapy Helen Singer Kaplan
The Pelican Freud Library
  Vol. 1 *Introductory Lectures on Psychoanalysis*
  Vol. 2 *New Introductory Lectures on Psychoanalysis*
  Vol. 3 *Studies on Hysteria* (with J. Breuer)
  Vol. 4 *The Interpretation of Dreams*
  Vol. 5 *The Psychopathology of Everyday Life*
  Vol. 6 *Jokes and Their Relation to the Unconscious*
  Vol. 7 *On Sexuality*
  Vol. 8 *Case Histories 1: 'Dora' and 'Little Hans'*
  Vol. 9 *Case Histories 2: The 'Rat Man', Schreber, The 'Wolf Man',
    A Case of Female Homosexuality*
  Vol. 10 *On Psychopathology*
  Vol. 11 *Metapsychology*